SULLIVAN
COUNTY

SULLIVAN COUNTY

A Bicentennial History in Images

JOHN CONWAY

THE History PRESS

Published by The History Press
Charleston, SC 29403
www.historypress.net

First published 2009

Manufactured in the United States

ISBN 978.1.59629.646.6

Library of Congress Cataloging-in-Publication Data

Conway, John, 1952-
Sullivan County : a bicentennial history in images / John Conway.
p. cm.
ISBN 978-1-59629-646-6
1. Sullivan County (N.Y.)--History. 2. Sullivan County (N.Y.)--History--Pictorial works.
I. Title.
F127.S91C67 2009
974.7'35--dc22
2009014468

CONTENTS

Acknowledgements		7
Introduction	Timber, Tanning and Tourism	9
Chapter 1	The Beginning	15
Chapter 2	The Transition	31
Chapter 3	The Silver Age	49
Chapter 4	Through the Depression to the Golden Age	81
Chapter 5	The Fortress Hotel	105
Chapter 6	After the Fall	117

ACKNOWLEDGEMENTS

Many people have assisted in the preparation of this book, beginning with Jonathan Simcosky and Kate Pluhar at The History Press. Their patience and guidance have been invaluable. The Sullivan County legislature, the county's bicentennial committee and legislative aide Alexis Eggleton provided the initial impetus. Many of my colleagues were helpful in supplying photos, including town historians Mary Curtis of Delaware, Frank V. Schwarz of Lumberland and Carole Smythe of Neversink. Other photos and direction came from Emily Hallock of the Tusten Historical Society; George Ardito and Robert Decker, past president and president, respectively, of the Sullivan County Historical Society; Rita Sheehan, Bethel town clerk; Virginia Lawrence and the Friends of the Beaverkill; Dan Hust and Fred Stabbert at the *Sullivan County Democrat*; and Yuri and Orest Blanarovich of the Mountain View Resort in Glen Spey. The time and effort they expended on my behalf is sincerely appreciated. Finally, the book would not have been possible without the assistance of my wife, Debbie, who freely and enthusiastically lent her own considerable talent and skill to this project.

Introduction

TIMBER, TANNING AND TOURISM

When Sullivan County was officially formed from Ulster County on March 27, 1809, it was a heavily forested, rocky and rugged region, largely inaccessible to the rest of the world. But the natural beauty of its many lakes, streams and rivers had already made it a very special place to a group of Native Americans who revered such features.

Some archaeologists believe that the Lenape (pronounced "len-ahh'-pay" and most often translated as "original people") first arrived in this area over eleven thousand years ago. While there is no indication exactly what the place was like at that time, oral tradition (the Lenape had no written language) holds that the tribe ultimately controlled a land mass that encompassed from what is today upstate New York to the state of Delaware. They called this land *Lenapehoking*, or "land of the Lenape."

The tribe spent the warm weather months in this heavily forested region, particularly along the major rivers, which they used for transportation. Here they hunted, fished and farmed, growing corn, squash and beans. They held great council fires in the Mamakating Valley and annual corn harvest festivals along the Delaware River at what is today Cochecton.

With the arrival of the Europeans—Swedish, Dutch and then British settlers—beginning in the middle of the seventeenth century, visits by the dwindling Lenape population became fewer and farther between. War and disease had severely diminished their numbers, and friction with the Europeans, who were anxious to purchase land (a concept totally alien to the Lenape), prompted the tribe to look elsewhere to live. By 1730, the Lenape people had left the region for good.

Soon, the area was abuzz with industry. Timber was abundant and in great demand. As early as 1764, a man named Daniel Skinner conceived the idea of floating the tall, sturdy pine trees that grew along the banks of the Delaware River to Philadelphia for use in the flourishing shipbuilding industry in that city. Timber rafting, the first of the county's three great industries—historians today call them the three *T*s—was born.

Brothers Samuel F. and John P. Jones founded the village of Monticello in 1804, and Samuel was instrumental in the construction of the Newburgh–Cochecton Turnpike, the first improved road through the county, and in the erection of the county itself. John P. Jones built the initial home in Monticello, cutting down the first tree himself in September 1804. When the new county was finally chiseled out of the southwestern corner of Ulster County and chartered in 1809, it was named for General John Sullivan, the Revolutionary War officer who had been directed by George Washington to drive the Mohawks and Tories, who had been raiding the settlements along the frontier, out of the region.

The Delaware & Hudson Canal, which opened in 1828 and was initially constructed to carry coal from the Moosic Mountains of Pennsylvania to the Hudson River for shipment to New York City, provided the first great population boom in the county. In fact, in the first twenty years of the canal's operation, the population of Sullivan County more than doubled, to more than twenty-five thousand by 1850.

The canal was also instrumental in the growth of the county's second great industry—tanning, which began in the 1830s and peaked during the Civil War, when the county's tanneries provided boots and other leather goods for the Union army.

Sullivan County hemlocks produced a peculiar, reddish-hued leather, which was stronger and suppler than that tanned elsewhere. At their height, the county's tanneries employed thousands of men, and Sullivan produced more leather than any other county. Entire communities grew up around these tanning operations, and many immigrants, especially from Ireland, came specifically to work in the trade.

The tanning industry thrived until the hemlock stands were depleted. By the end of the 1880s, all but one of the forty tanneries in the county had vanished, and for the most part, so had the massive fortunes amassed by those who owned them.

When the landscape of Sullivan County had been drastically altered by the timber and tanning industries, the area turned to tourism (the third *T*) as its principal industry. Beginning in the 1840s, entrepreneurs were building summer hotels to accommodate visitors, who, having learned of the great recreational opportunities here from writers such as Alfred B. Street and Charles Fenno Hoffman and painters such as Henry Inman, came here to fish and hunt.

John Beekman Finlay built the first hotel specifically for summer tourists in White Lake around 1845, and David B. Kinne followed by constructing the Mansion House nearby in 1848. As the end of the nineteenth century approached, small resorts had replaced logging camps and farmhouses had become boardinghouses. With the railroads providing easy access to the county for the first time, the tourism industry really began to grow.

The western side of the county along the Delaware River began to develop first, with the completion of the Erie Railroad in 1850. The railroad embarked on an aggressive promotional campaign, touting the upper Delaware region as "a sportsmen's paradise," and small hotels played host to those looking for recreation and an escape from the oppressive summer heat of the cities.

The Erie also provided a boost to the burgeoning bluestone industry in the river valley, which had until then been utilizing the canal to ship stone to New York City for curbs, sidewalks and foundations. While the canal had to shut down its operation during the coldest winter months, the railroad ran year-round, and the bluestone industry enjoyed a meteoric boon.

When the center of the county got rail service with the completion of the Monticello & Port Jervis Railroad in 1871 and the New York & Oswego Midland Railroad (later the Ontario & Western) in 1872, resorts began to spring up there as well. Soon, thousands of visitors a year were spending their summers in the cool and health-restoring mountains. The O&W, especially, enthusiastically promoted the region—and its healing environment—in its annual vacation guides.

From 1890 to about 1915, the county enjoyed an unparalleled prosperity as about two hundred hotels—such as the Wawonda, the Swannanoa and Ye Lancashire Inn in Liberty; the Leona Hotel, the Lawrence House and the White Sulphur Springs House in White Sulphur Springs; the Columbia Farms, Applebee Inn and Brophy's Mountain House in Hurleyville; and the Mansion House, the Prospect House and the Kenmore Hotel in White Lake—thrived.

These hotels were largely wood-frame buildings of Victorian architecture and were all gentile owned. While at first they offered their guests simply fresh air, clean water, farm fresh vegetables and milk and plenty of shade, by 1895 lawn tennis had become an attraction, and by 1897 golf was offered. The county's first hotel golf course was opened that year at the Trout Valley Farm on the Beaverkill, and several more, including three official nine-hole courses, followed by 1901.

Vacationers who flocked to Sullivan County during this Silver Age came for the same reasons that the Lenape first visited the area centuries before—to enjoy the fresh air, the clean water and the magnificent scenery.

The railroads had long promoted the fresh mountain air of Sullivan County as a cure for people suffering from tuberculosis (or consumption, as it was widely known at the time), and a number of treatment facilities were built in the county, most notably the Loomis Sanitarium just outside Liberty. Hotel owners blamed the county's budding reputation as a haven for those afflicted with tuberculosis for destroying their business, and by 1915 many of the once magnificent hotels had closed. A number of them soon burned to the ground.

The county had already begun a radical change. A seasonal influx of New York City–based Jewish immigrants began with a boardinghouse built by John Gerson in Rock Hill in 1899. Soon, other Jewish families had purchased struggling hotels. Still others came to farm but soon found that they could make more by entertaining friends and relatives in the spare rooms than from the soil. This provided Jewish vacationers, unwelcome in many other resort areas, a place to spend their free time in the company of other Jews. Most notable among these early Jewish hoteliers were Selig and Malke Grossinger in Liberty (1914), the Kutsher family near Monticello (1907) and Fleischer and Morganstern, who purchased the Flagler House in Fallsburg (1908).

Another type of resort was created by wealthy urban sportsmen, with Chester W. Chapin owning more than twenty thousand acres covering several towns and William Howe Crane forming the Hartwood Club in Forestburgh. Economist Henry George founded what became a mecca for artists at Merriewold Park in 1889. Meanwhile, the Willowemoc and Beaverkill remained major fly-fishing destinations.

The Jewish immigrants built large hotels in places like Fallsburg, Liberty and Livingston Manor. Inspired by Fleischer and Morganstern's Flagler, the area's preeminent resort at the time, hotel owners soon popularized a new style of architecture—featuring stucco exteriors, palladium windows, multiple façades and prominent parapets—that became known as Sullivan County Mission. By the 1940s, over three hundred hotels were in operation in Sullivan County. The Golden Age had begun and would last for about twenty-five very prosperous years.

By 1953, the *New York Times* reported that there were 538 hotels in the county, including 2 of the most famous resorts in the world: Grossinger's in Liberty and the Concord in Kiamesha Lake. At the same time, the paper noted that the county's accommodations also included 1,000 rooming houses and 50,000 bungalows.

By this time, the major resorts were offering their guests modern amenities, such as golf, tennis, indoor and outdoor swimming pools and skating rinks, professional entertainment and three hearty meals a day, instead of merely the fresh air and clean water of days gone by. Still, hardly an afternoon would pass when thousands of summer tourists wouldn't take to the country roads for a stroll in the magnificent countryside.

This era of prosperity lasted until about 1965. Many factors played a role in the decline of the Catskill resorts. The growth of suburbia and the proliferation of air conditioning made summers in the city more bearable. Inexpensive air travel opened up new horizons to middle- and working-class vacationers, and Jewish families became assimilated. Sullivan County resorts, which had survived for decades by constantly evolving—adding tennis, golf, swimming pools, indoor swimming pools, nightclubs, harness racing, etc.—suddenly failed to adjust. Sullivan County had fallen on hard economic times by the 1970s, and no simple solution was at hand.

Meanwhile, in August 1969, about 500,000 young people from all over the country converged on an alfalfa field in Bethel for a three-day event that was planned for a fraction of that number. Heavy rains and inadequate facilities did little to dampen the enthusiasm of the crowd, which enjoyed "three days of peace and music." This event, the Woodstock Music Festival, helped define a generation, but despite a number of half-hearted attempts, the county was mostly unable to commercially capitalize on this claim to fame. In fact, for many years after the festival, it seemed as if county officials, as well as many residents, would have preferred that the concert had never taken place. The traffic jams that paralyzed the region, destruction of private property and garbage left in the festival's aftermath resulted in a bad taste in the mouths of many residents. The county board of supervisors enacted a strict mass gathering law to prevent a recurrence.

Now, as Sullivan County celebrates its 200th birthday, its landscape continuing to evolve with the disappearance of the large hotels of the Golden Age, vacationers continue to flock to the area to enjoy its rich natural beauty, recreational opportunities and a renewed appreciation for the significance of Woodstock.

Tourism continues to be the county's primary industry, and while a few hotels resembling, superficially at least, the resorts of the past remain in operation, bed-and-breakfasts provide the most accommodations, and many visitors today own or rent second homes here. These visitors, who come year-round, play golf, ski, look for the bald eagles that inhabit the county and enjoy new tourist attractions.

The concert venue at Bethel Woods, the site of the original Woodstock Music Festival, is world class and improves with each year of operation. The newly created Museum at Bethel Woods commemorates not just the music festival, but also the decade of the 1960s and the changes its events brought to the country. Local billionaire Alan Gerry has spared no expense in painstakingly creating these complementary venues.

A new concept in tourism, the Monticello Motor Club, began operation in 2008. The facility, which is expected to eventually include an elaborate clubhouse and other luxurious amenities, features a state-of-the-art road-racing course open only to club members. A six-figure initiation fee and pricey annual dues ensure an exclusive membership.

Harkening back to the environmental stewardship of the Lenape, and true to its historical development, in which the appreciation of nature played a significant role, Sullivan County has begun to tout itself as a center of "green" technology. Plans have been developed for a "green technology industrial park," and local start-ups include a company that specializes in building, selling and repairing electric and other alternative fuel vehicles.

Many residents hold on to the hope for casino gaming, and Empire Resorts, which has been operating the Monticello Gaming and Raceway facility, has partnered with developer Louis Cappelli to propose an extravagant entertainment complex at the site of the fabled Concord Hotel.

Time marches on, but in the past, present and future, Sullivan County remains a very special place.

Chapter 1

THE BEGINNING

The Lenape referred to the earliest European settlers arriving in *Lenapehoking* as *shawunnuck*, or "salty people," because of the Algonquin tradition that the white man had been created from the salt water of the ocean beating on the shores of Europe and the foam, thus formed, eventually drifted here to North America. Many of these early settlers sought the riches that were long rumored to abound in the region. Others came to make a living from the natural bounty of the land—trapping animals for fur or cutting timber for sale elsewhere.

These first Europeans discovered an unspoiled frontier, rich in natural beauty and resources. As late as 1779, the upper Delaware Valley was so primitive that it was, as described by historian Isabel Thompson Kelsay, writing about the Battle of Minisink in her book *Joseph Brant: Man of Two Worlds*, "a howling wilderness."

"There was not a wilder, lonelier place on the whole frontier," she wrote, "a place where the wolves gathered by night but men were seldom seen."

James Eldridge Quinlan writes in his *History of Sullivan County* that when the brothers Samuel F. and John P. Jones first arrived in the area they called Monticello, there was nothing much there except swamp and laurel. It was so overgrown, in fact, that the brothers became separated on their initial visit and almost perished before finding each other.

Quinlan also notes that the area known as Hurleyville, which founder William Hurley envisioned as becoming the county's third great community (after Thompsonville and Monticello), was populated mainly by "muskrats, raccoons, and foxes" as late as the mid-nineteenth century.

When the county was finally formed in 1809, the first order of business was to designate a county seat, and after much political maneuvering, Monticello was chosen. The choice was not a universally popular one, however, and it took the board of supervisors nearly two years to approve monies to erect the county buildings.

The bounty of the land provided the area's first industries: timber was rafted down the Delaware to Philadelphia (and elsewhere along the river) for use in the shipbuilding industry, and bluestone was shipped to New York for construction there. Sawmills and gristmills were erected on virtually every stream of any size, and eventually other small industries were developed, including knife making and the manufacture of scoops and hoops.

The tanning industry, which had been thriving in neighboring Ulster County since about 1815, arrived in Sullivan in the early 1830s. One of the first tanneries was built by John Eldridge in Thompson in 1831, and another was built by Rufus Palen in Fallsburg that same year. The abundance of hemlock trees in the region encouraged many tanners to locate here, and soon entire communities—Stevensville, Stevensburgh, Mongaup Valley and Gilmans among them—had grown up around the tanneries.

Curiously, even while the natural beauty of the region was being altered by these early industries, a tourism industry, comprising mainly fishermen and other nature lovers, began to develop, though very slowly at first. As incongruous as it may seem, this fledgling industry managed to coexist with the other, seemingly incompatible activities, providing a subtle portent of what was to come.

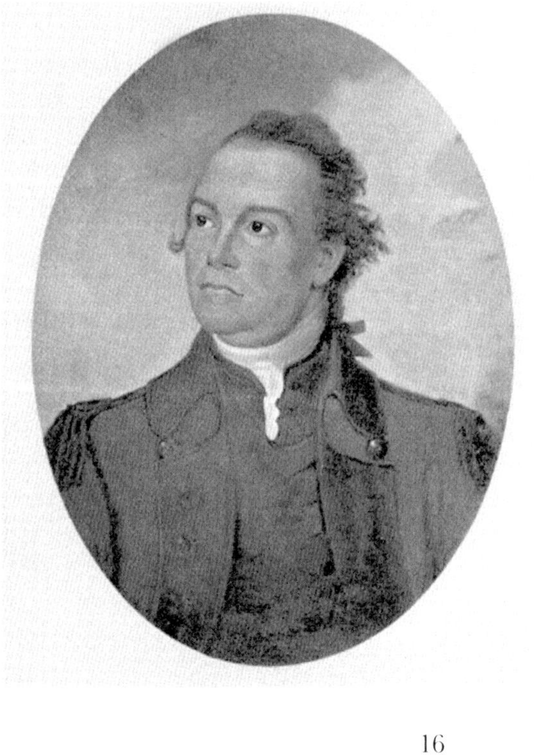

When the new county was formed in 1809, residents wanted to name it for a Revolutionary War hero. General John Sullivan, who later was governor of New Hampshire, was chosen because he had driven the Mohawks and Tories off the frontier that had included the Delaware, Neversink and Mamakating Valleys.

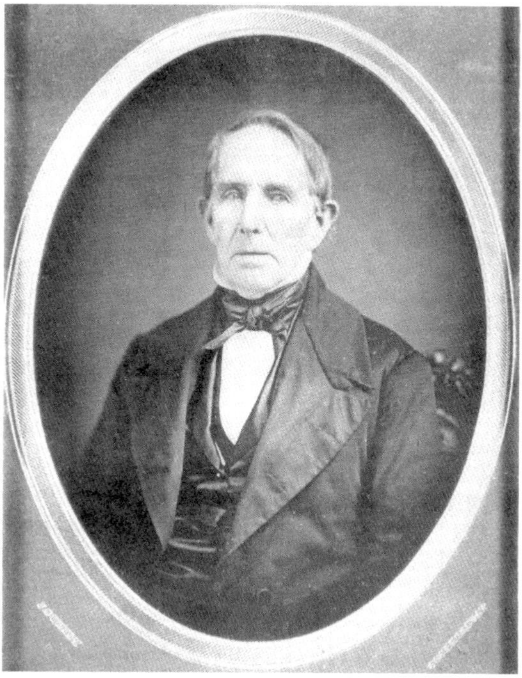

Right: John Patterson Jones (pictured) and his older brother, Samuel Frisbee Jones, founders of the village of Monticello, were among the early leaders in the county. Samuel almost single-handedly procured for his village the designation as county seat, and John held many offices, including state senator.

Below: John Patterson Jones built the first house in Monticello in 1804. Though not an expert axe man, he cut down the first tree himself. The house was located on the southeast corner of Main and Mill Streets, or present-day Broadway and St. John.

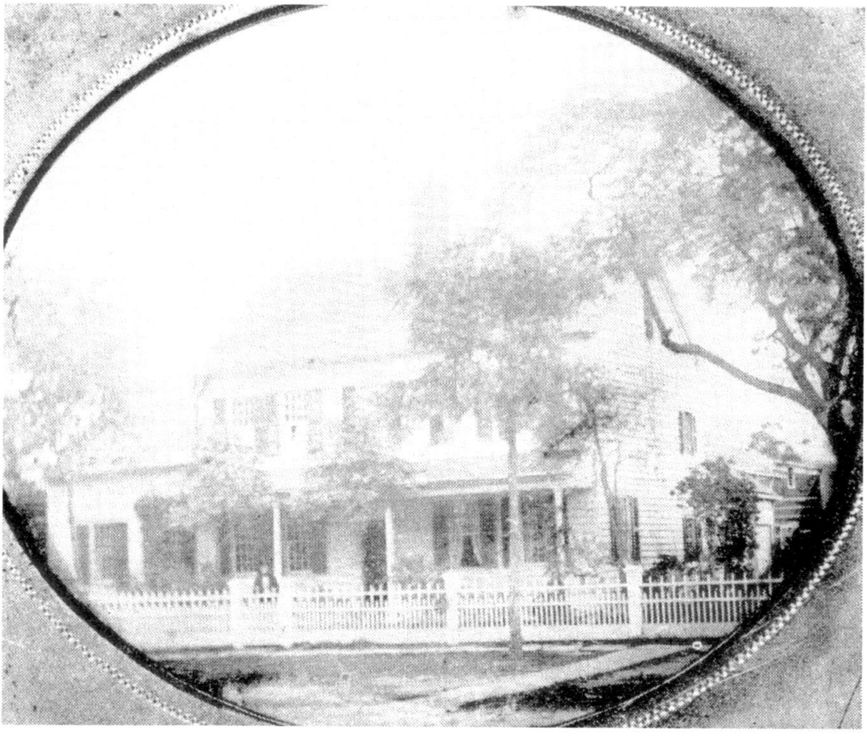

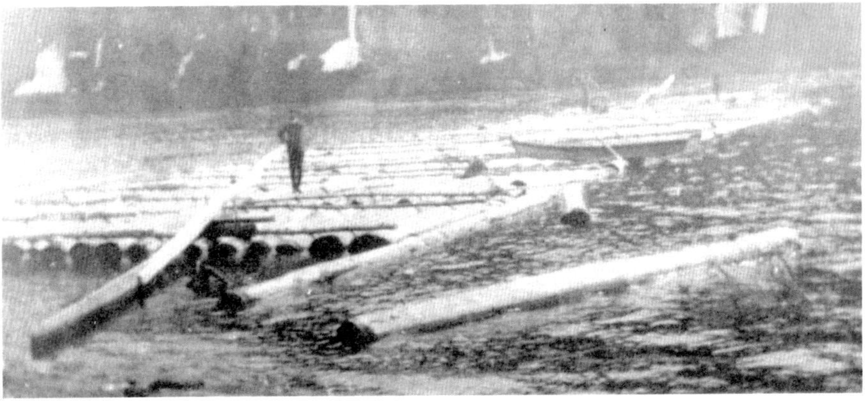

Timber rafting was the region's first great industry, predating the county itself. Daniel Skinner rafted the first lumber to Philadelphia in 1764, and the industry peaked in the mid-nineteenth century, also spawning the first inns along the Delaware River, which provided raftsmen with food and accommodations on their journey.

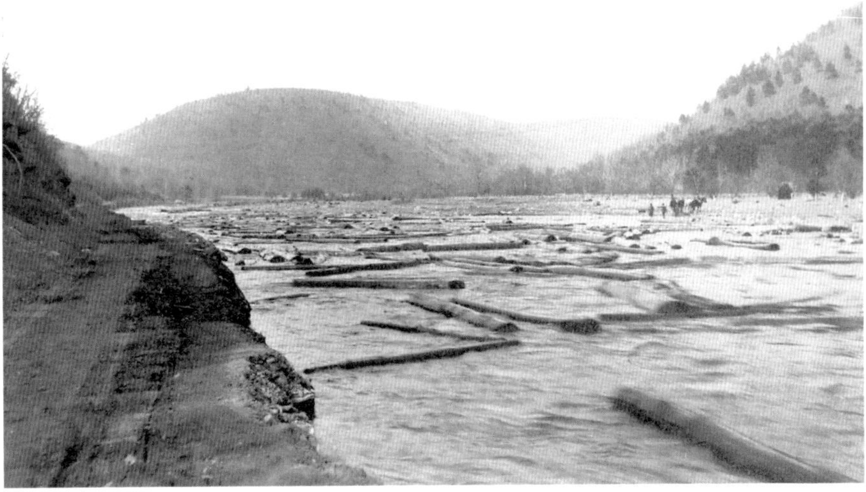

While at first only select softwoods were cut for the shipbuilding industry, soon virtually everything was being harvested, and streams throughout the county were utilized to get the timber to the Delaware. Here, individual logs float near Narrowsburg. *Photo courtesy of the Tusten Historical Society, Narrowsburg.*

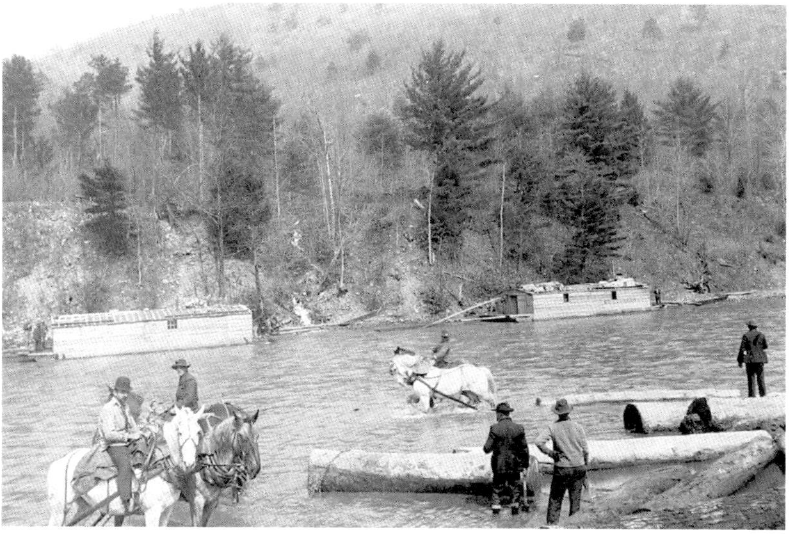

Timber was a tough trade, and loggers worked long days. While stockpiling logs for rafting, they would often take their meals on the river. The crude floating structures in the photo are where they would eat their noontime meal. *Photo courtesy of the Tusten Historical Society, Narrowsburg.*

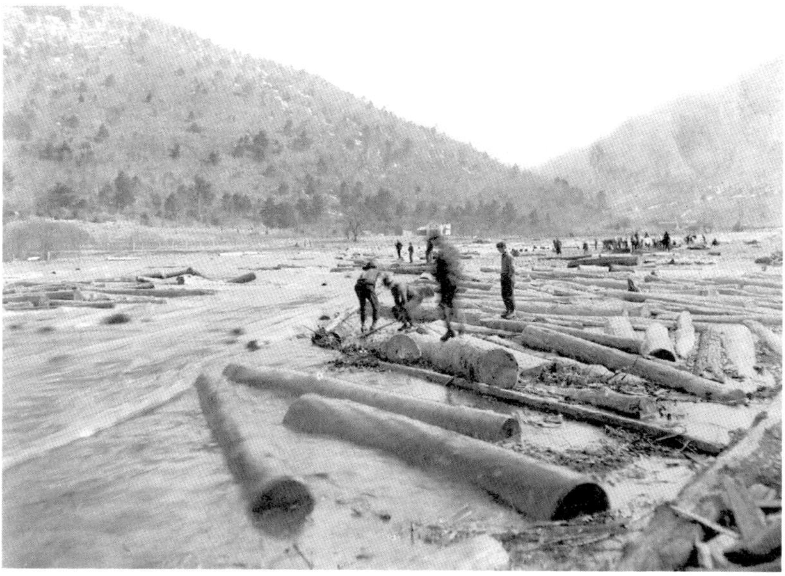

Since the feeder streams varied in size, most often individual logs or small rafts called colts were floated to the banks of the Delaware, where they would be stockpiled for construction of the larger river rafts. Timber rafting was a viable industry, though on a much smaller scale, into the early 1900s. *Photo courtesy of the Tusten Historical Society, Narrowsburg.*

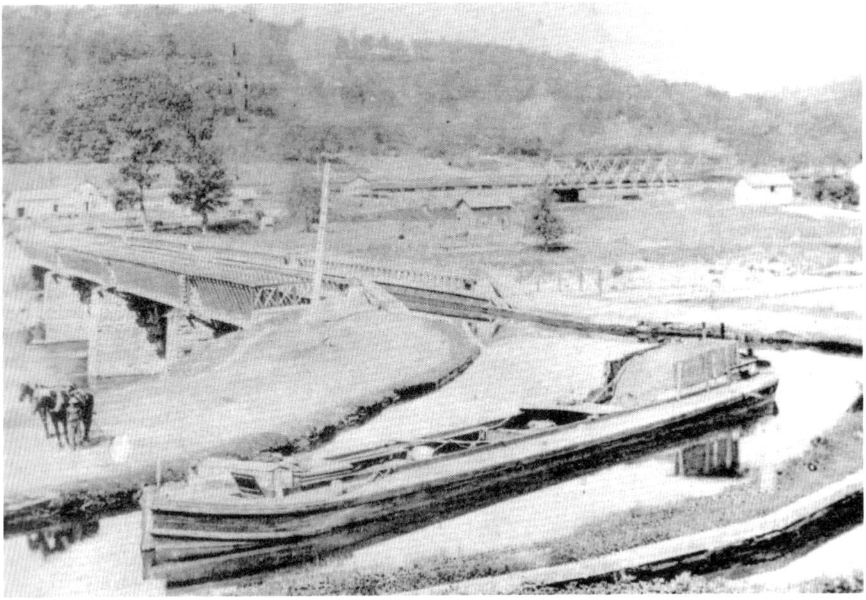

The D&H Canal was built to take coal from the Moosic Mountains of Pennsylvania to New York City via the Hudson River, but its economic impact on Sullivan County was considerable. Canalboats were not powered in any way. They were pulled by horses or mules, which in turn were most often led by children.

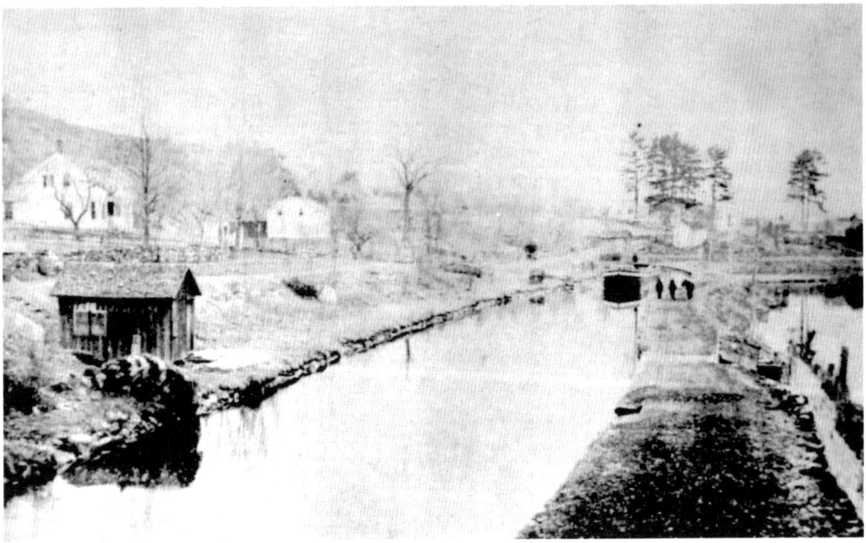

The D&H Canal took three years to build, opened in 1828 and operated until 1898. It was 108 miles long and, coincidentally, featured 108 locks.

Right: John A. Roebling, who designed the Delaware Aqueduct on the canal, as well as several others, was a bridge-building engineer who pioneered the concept of wire rope suspension in the United States. When the Delaware Aqueduct opened in 1848, it signaled a new era in the canal's existence.

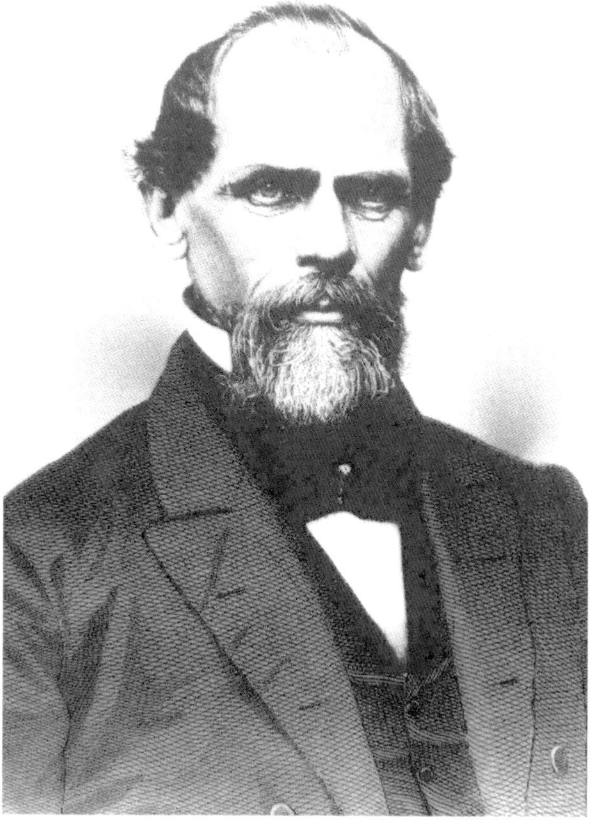

Below: The Delaware Aqueduct carried the canal over the river, precluding the canalboats from having to contend with the current, allowing the canal company to remove the dam from the river and preventing the all-too-frequent mishaps between canalboats and timber rafts.

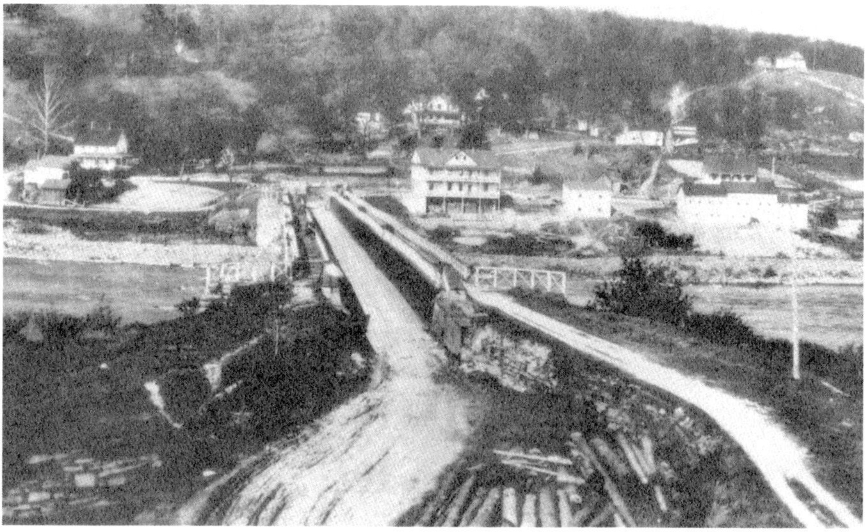

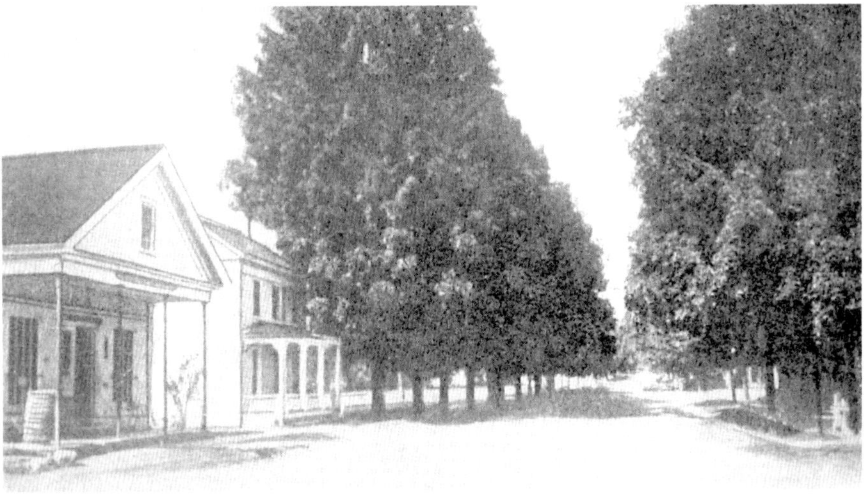

Wurtsboro, previously known as Rome, was one of several Sullivan County communities that grew up around the D&H Canal and was named for Maurice Wurts, one of the three Wurts brothers involved in the construction and operation of the canal, who resided there for a time.

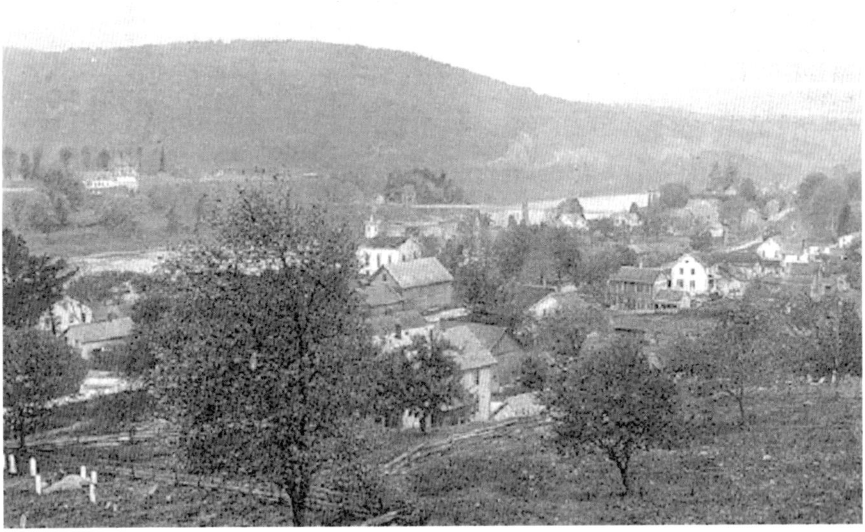

Barryville, founded around 1830 and named for William T. Barry, the nation's first postmaster general, owed its existence to the canal, which operated several businesses there. Barryville had a population of about three hundred in 1844, when the county's board of supervisors seriously considered moving the county seat there.

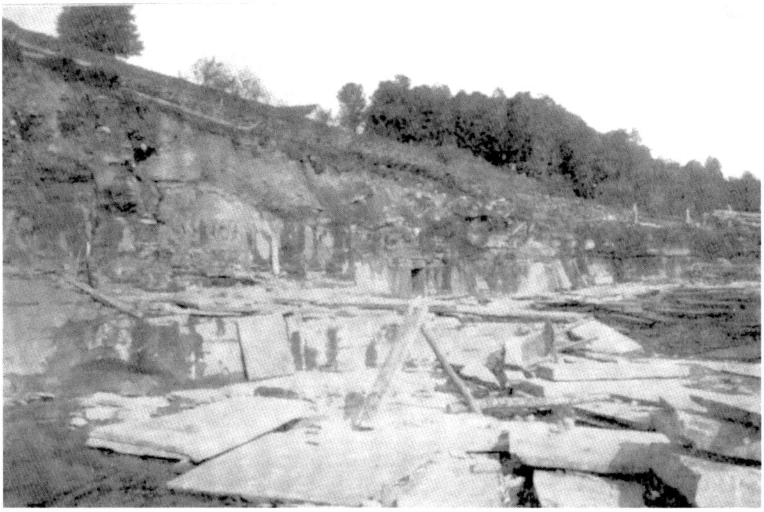

Although it never reached the proportions that it attained in neighboring Ulster County, bluestone quarrying was, for a time, a leading industry in Sullivan. The first quarry in the county was discovered by accident by local rattlesnake hunter Steve Griffin. Other men, such as John F. Kilgour, made millions in the business, but most lost their fortunes in the risky venture.

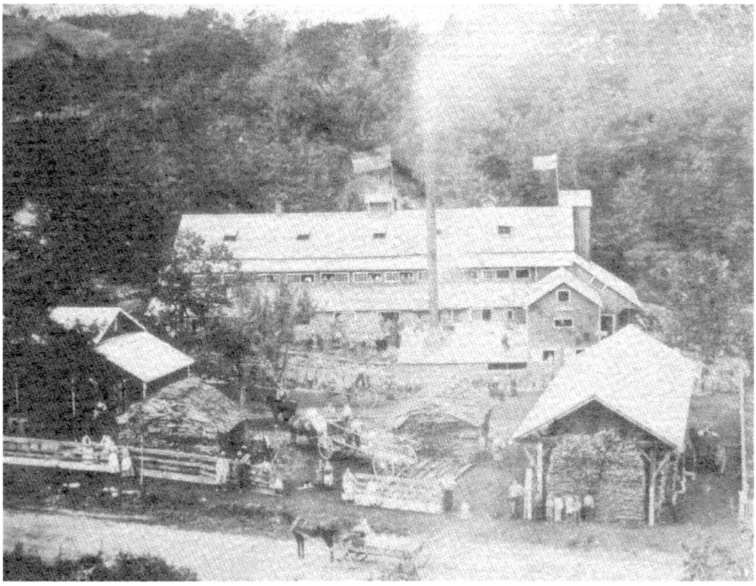

Leather tanning became the county's second great industry beginning in 1831. During the Civil War, Sullivan tanned more leather than any other county. Most of the tanneries tanned sole leather, as did the Wurtsboro Tannery (pictured) until it was converted to tan upper leather and French calfskin in 1865.

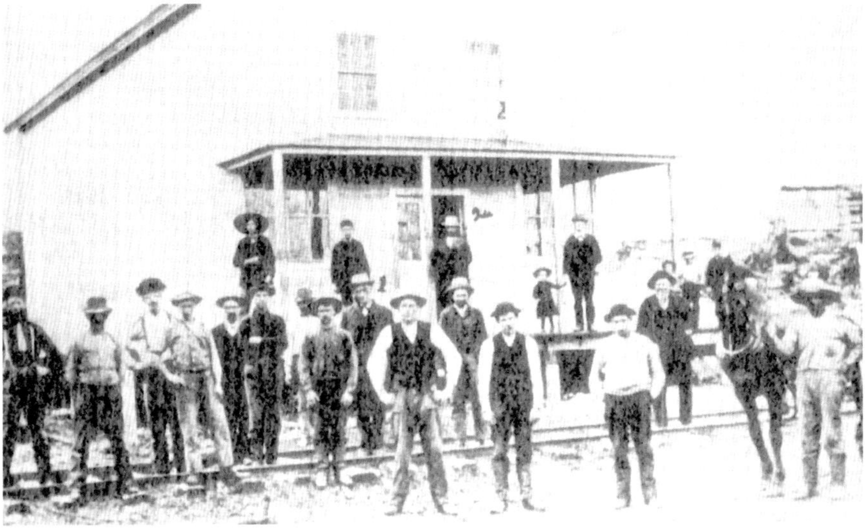

Workers pose outside one of the buildings at Gilmans, the community that grew up around the tannery and gang sawmill of W.W. Gilman, the eccentric multimillionaire who amassed over three thousand acres in the town of Forestburgh. W.W. Gilman died in 1885.

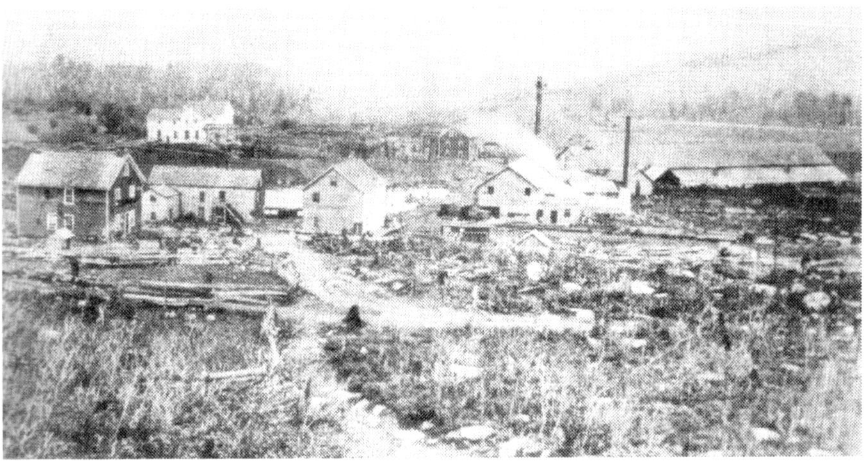

The railroad depot was attached to Gilmans's sawmill operation to make it easier to ship the finished lumber. Gilmans became an important stop on the Monticello & Port Jervis Railroad until much of the community was destroyed in a fire in May 1884. The station later became known as St. Joseph's.

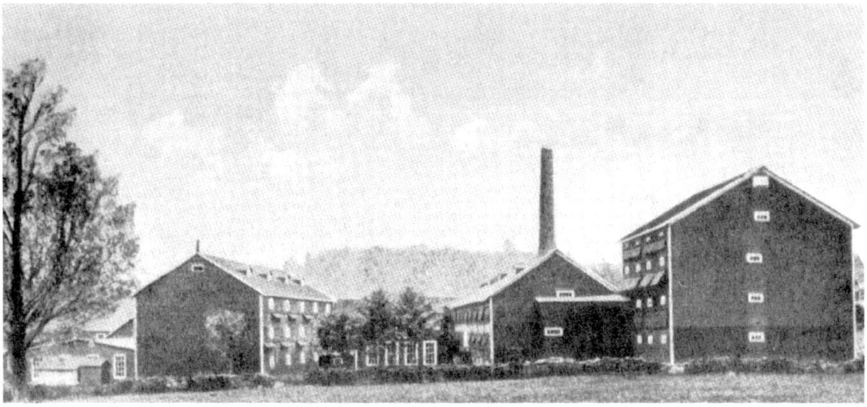

The tannery in Monticello was the only tanning operation in Sullivan County to survive into the twentieth century. It was built by Ephraim Burnham and later operated by Strong, Starr & Company, tanning primarily book leather. It burned down in 1924.

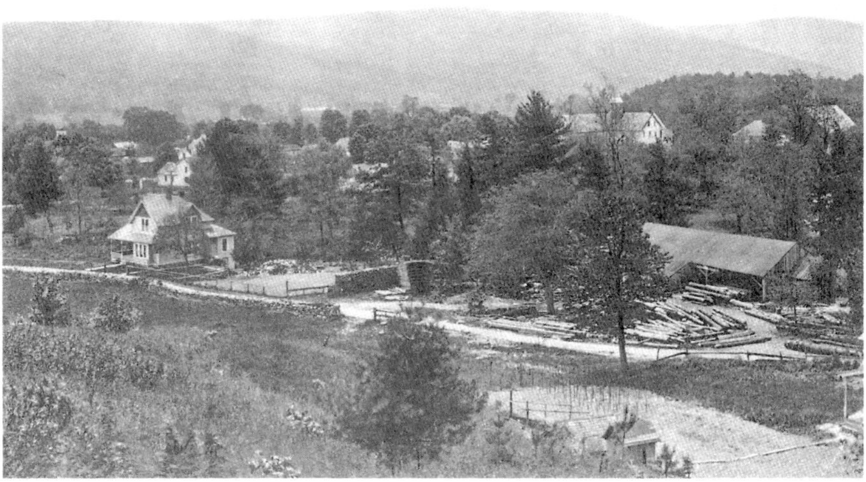

Helm's Mill in Wurtsboro was fairly typical of the mills that evolved from the earliest up-and-down sawmills in the county.

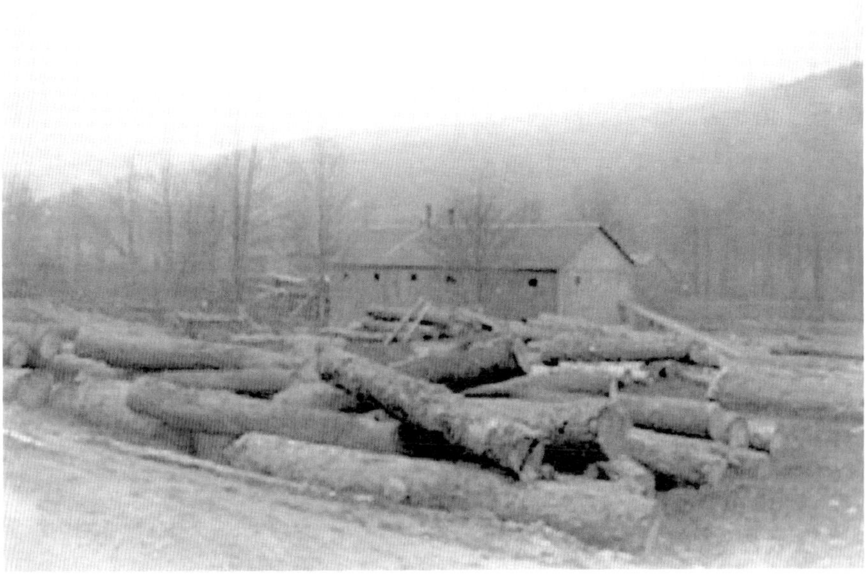

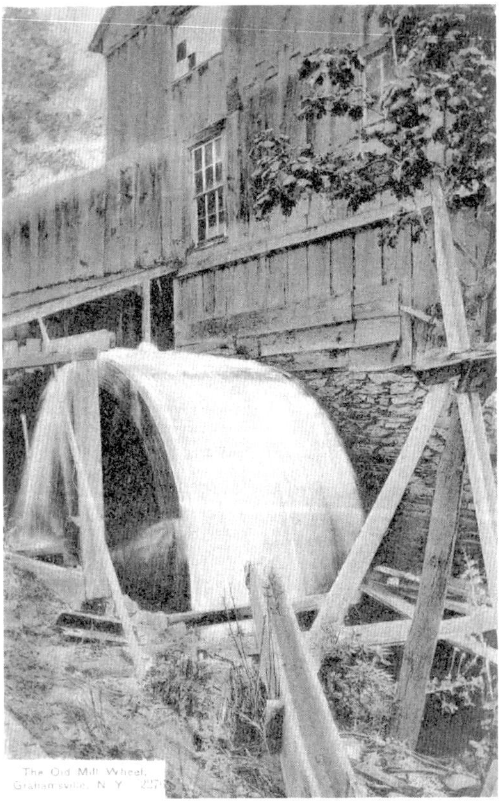

Above: Logs awaiting their fate outside the Beaverkill sawmill, which operated for a number of years adjacent to one of America's most famous trout streams.

Left: Grahamsville, named in memory of Lieutenant John Graham, a local militia officer killed by Mohawks in the skirmish at Chestnut Woods in 1778, featured a number of small industries, including this mill. *Photo courtesy of Time and the Valleys Museum, Grahamsville.*

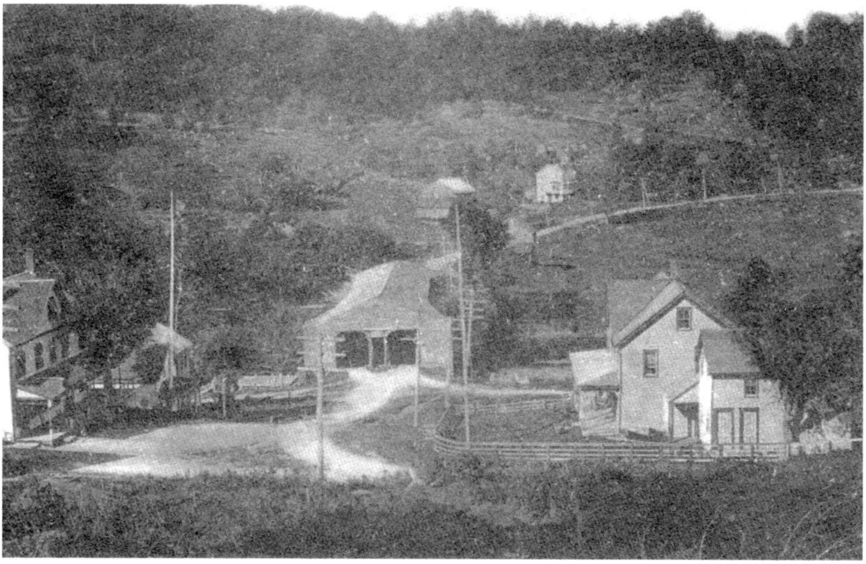

The covered bridge from which Bridgeville took its name was designed and built in 1807 by Major Salmon Wheat, an Orange County farmer. It was New York State's first covered bridge and stood for 116 years.

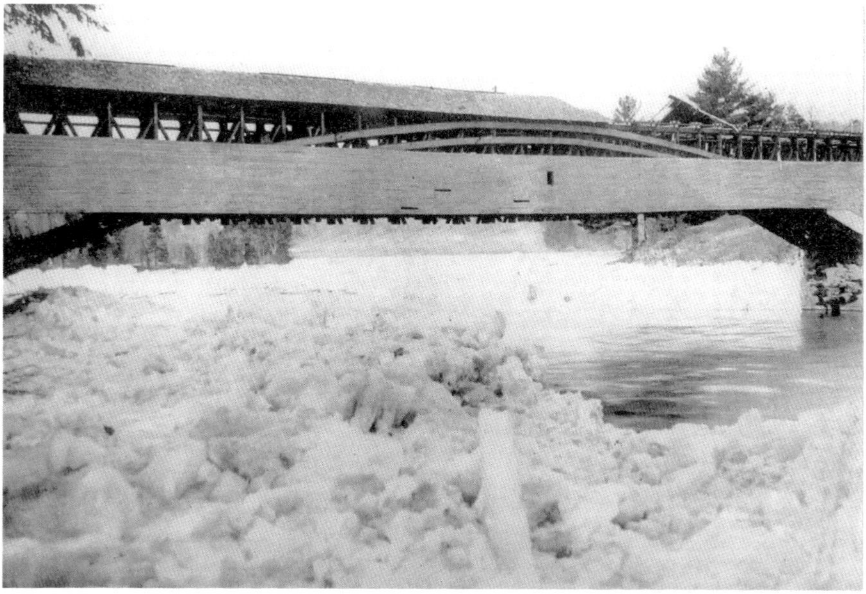

The original covered bridge at Narrowsburg, the first span from New York to Pennsylvania in the upper Delaware region, was built in 1811. It was rebuilt after it was destroyed by ice in 1832 and again when it was destroyed by a flood in 1846. A covered bridge served Narrowsburg until 1899. *Photo courtesy of the Tusten Historical Society, Narrowsburg.*

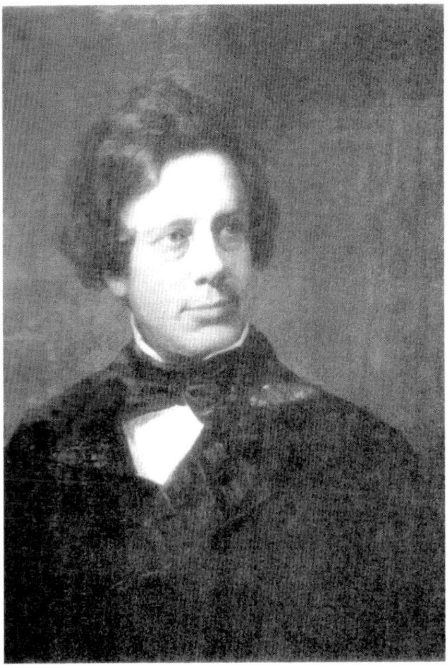

Left: Henry Inman was one of America's most prominent portrait painters when he turned to landscapes. A passionate fisherman, his paintings, most notably *Trout Fishing in Sullivan County*, helped draw attention to the recreational opportunities to be found in Sullivan County.

Below: Inman's oil on canvas *Trout Fishing in Sullivan County* (1841) has been called his most renowned landscape effort, as well as his most autobiographical. It likely depicts a section of the Beaverkill.

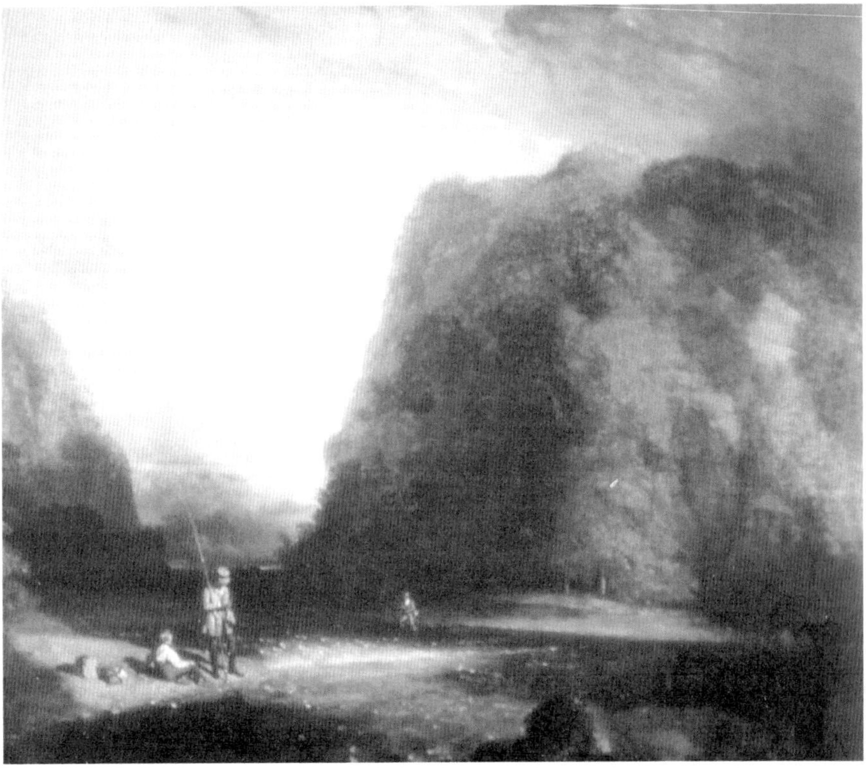

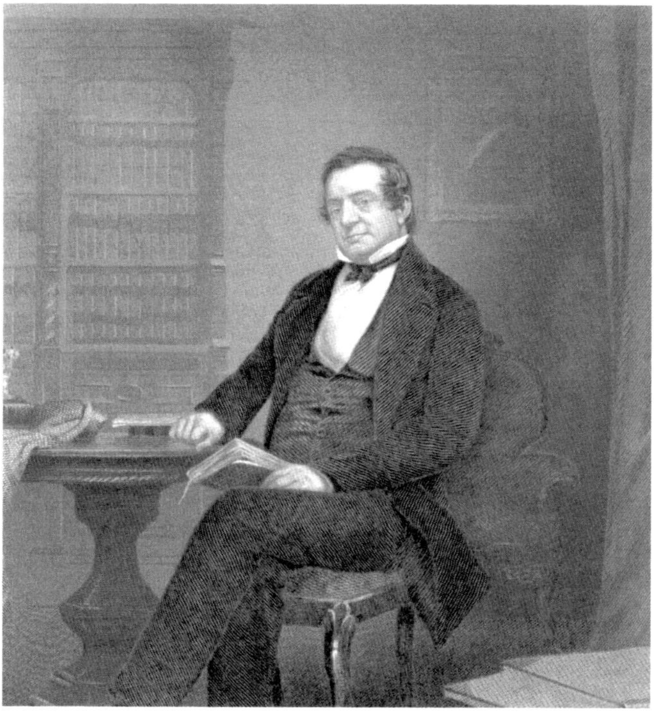

Washington Irving traveled through the county around 1834 and wrote glowingly of its beauty. He was especially taken with the journey over the Shawangunks from Bloomingburgh to Wurtsboro and set his 1838 short story "Hans Swartz: A Marvelous Tale of Mamakating Hollow" in that vicinity.

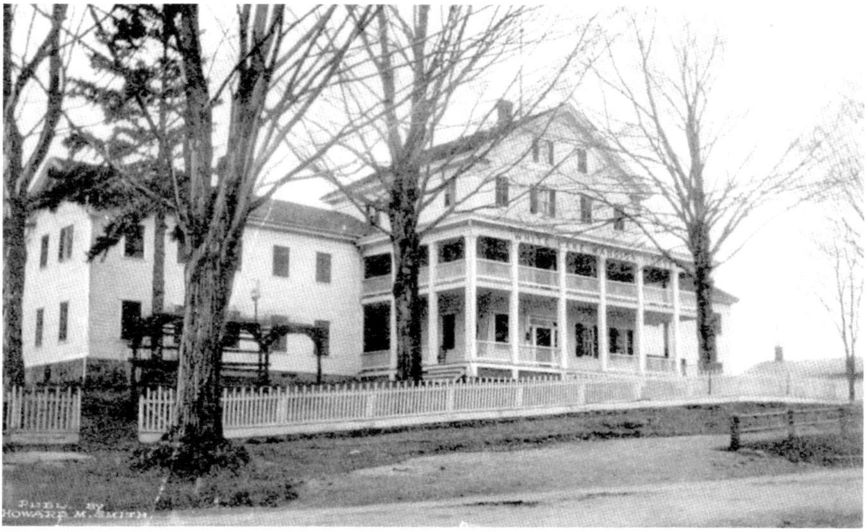

The influx of fishermen and other tourists to the county led entrepreneur John Beekman Finlay to construct the first hotel specifically for summer boarders in White Lake around 1845. David B. Kinne followed suit, building the nearby White Lake Mansion House (pictured) in 1848. It remains the oldest hotel still standing in the county. *Photo courtesy of Rita Sheehan, Bethel town clerk.*

Chapter 2
THE TRANSITION

Beginning at about the time the Civil War ended, Sullivan County entered into a prolonged period of great transition. The tanning industry had peaked during the war, but the end of the hostilities had, at least to some extent, lessened the great demand for leather. Simultaneously, the hemlock trees that were integral to the tanning process were rapidly being depleted. By the middle of the 1880s, all but one of the tanneries in the county had closed.

Like the rest of the country, the county contracted railroad fever, and soon rails were traversing the region, linking the mountains to the metropolitan New York area. Three railroads would eventually service the region, and their presence revolutionized life in the area.

The Erie Railroad, which had been completed through the county by 1850, began an aggressive promotional campaign, touting the upper Delaware region as "a sportsmen's paradise." Small hotels in places like Barryville, Glen Spey and Narrowsburg were soon hosting thousands of visitors each weekend.

The O&W Railroad, which serviced the interior of the county, used a different tactic, promoting instead the invigorating mountain air. "Doctors say, 'go to the mountains!'" their promotions hailed. As a result, hotels were built by entrepreneurs around most of the train stations. Some of these establishments were fancier than others, but they all enjoyed a symbiotic relationship with the railroad, which regularly offered to ship construction supplies for free if hotel owners would add to their accommodations.

The railroads also provided a new and better outlet for farmers. Dairy farms thrived, and creameries sprang up throughout the area. By April 1879, the railroad was running regular milk trains from Sullivan County, and the typical train made twenty-seven separate stops in the forty-nine miles from Morsston to Middletown, ending up with 250 cans of milk.

When the Sullivan County Milk Association was formed in 1880, there were about 2,500 dairy cows producing in the county, including 400 served by the Winterton station, 300 by Bloomingburg, 237 by Fallsburg and Centreville stations, 450 by the Liberty station, 436 by Parksville, 180 by Morsston and 339 by Livingston Manor. By the end of the following year, the railroad was transporting 17,430 cans of milk from the area each week, along with 165 cans of condensed milk and 311 cans of cream.

The railroads also provided other kinds of work. The stations had to be manned by ticket agents and freight handlers. Rudimentary security had to be provided. And, at least in the early days, ice had to be harvested to keep the trains running and to provide crude refrigeration.

Boosted by the railroads, the tourist trade that had begun around 1840 with visits by fishermen began to blossom. Writers and painters spread the word about the natural beauty of the area, as well as the recreational opportunities here. The poet Alfred B. Street, especially, was unrestrained in his praise of the wild and diffuse bounty that Mother Nature had bestowed on the county.

By the 1890s, the transition was complete. Once a desolate, industrialized region, Sullivan County had become a renowned tourist destination, boasting two hundred or so hotels offering summer visitors fresh air and plenty of shade, along with clean water and farm fresh produce. The Silver Age was at hand.

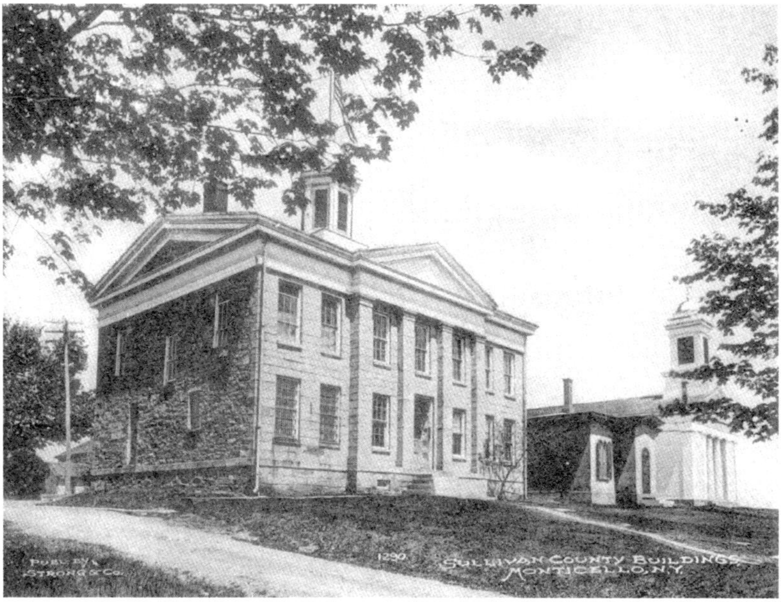

The original Sullivan County Courthouse burned down in 1844 and was replaced by this stone structure shortly thereafter. The fire also destroyed the clerk's office and prompted the county's supervisors to revisit the issue of locating the county seat. Because of divided opposition, with Liberty, Forestburgh, Barryville and Fallsburgh all vying for consideration, Monticello was able to retain its designation.

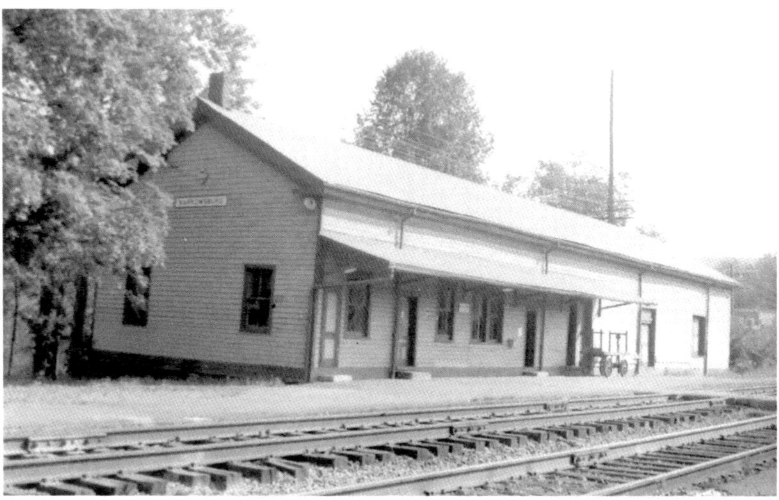

The Erie Railroad was complete through Sullivan County by 1850. Forced to run its tracks on the Pennsylvania side of the river north of Sparrow Bush, the Erie crossed back into New York at Delaware Bridge, just below Narrowsburg. This is the second Narrowsburg station. *Photo courtesy of the Tusten Historical Society, Narrowsburg*

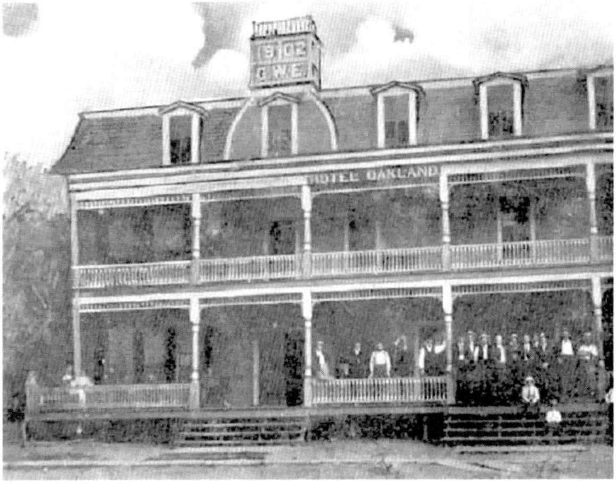

Narrowsburg was, for a time, the most important upper Delaware stop on the Erie, since everyone traveling to Hawley or Honesdale had to get off there. A number of hotels, including the Oakland (pictured), operated in the hamlet for that reason. When the railroad built its branch line into Pennsylvania, these hotels struggled, only to be reborn later as tourists flocked to the area. *Photo courtesy of the Tusten Historical Society, Narrowsburg.*

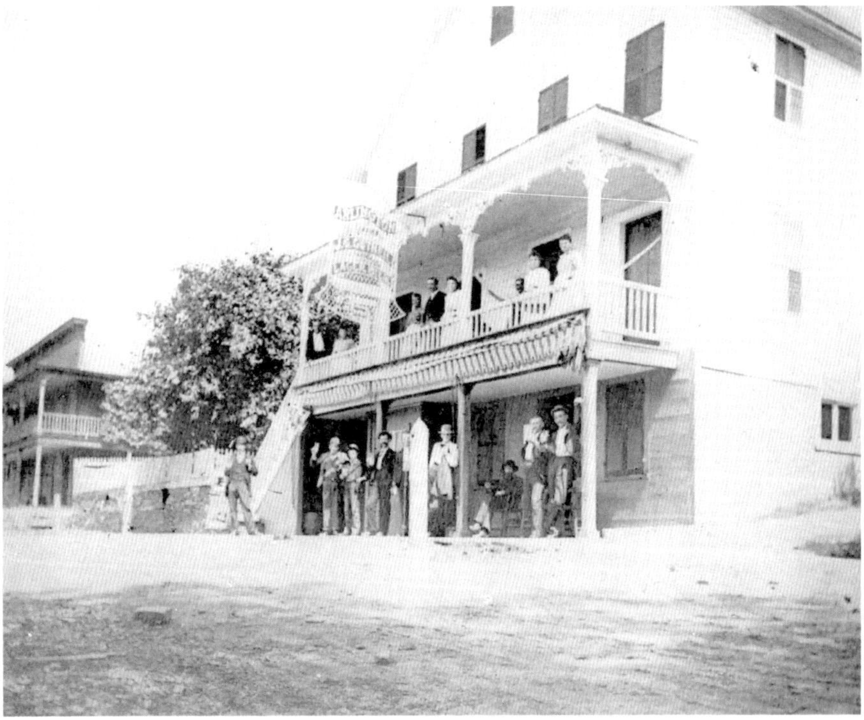

The original Arlington Hotel in Narrowsburg burned down in 1893. *Photo courtesy of the Tusten Historical Society, Narrowsburg.*

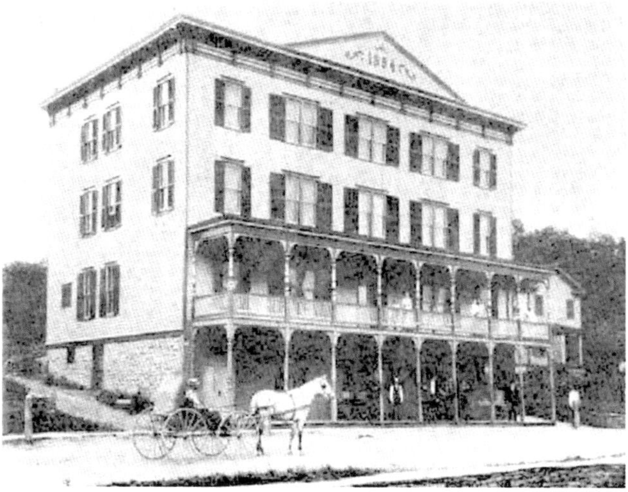

The new Arlington Hotel was built in 1894. It is now home to the Delaware Valley Arts Alliance. *Photo courtesy of the Tusten Historical Society, Narrowsburg.*

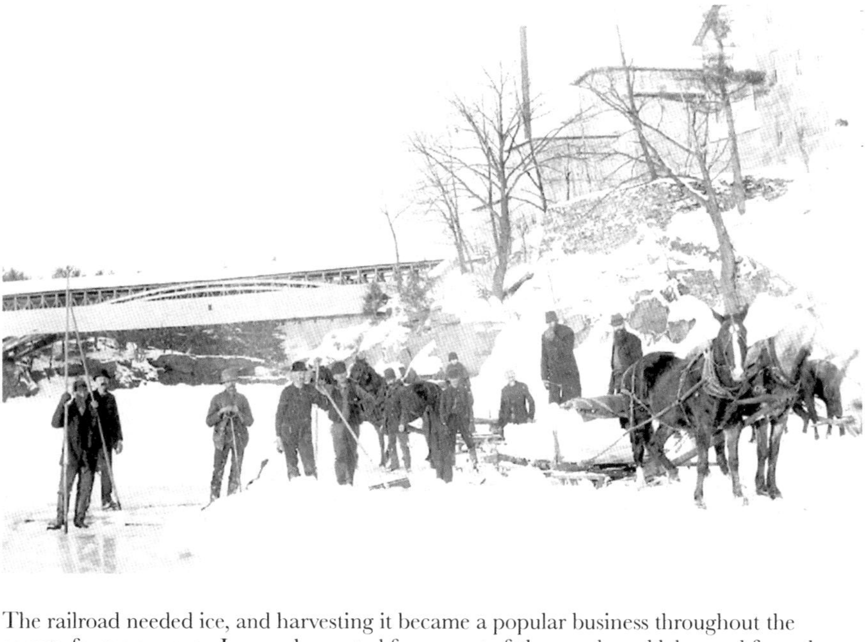

The railroad needed ice, and harvesting it became a popular business throughout the county for many years. Ice was harvested from most of the ponds and lakes and from the Delaware, as shown here with the Narrowsburg covered bridge in the background. *Photo courtesy of the Tusten Historical Society, Narrowsburg.*

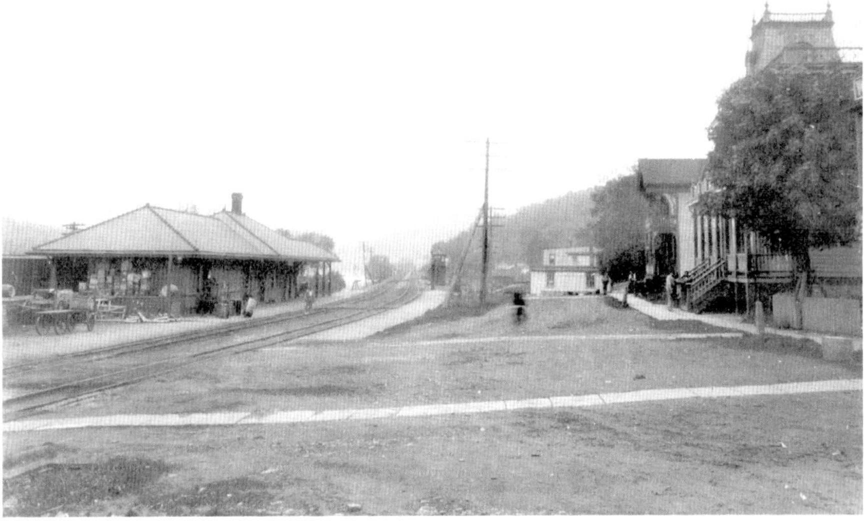

The Erie station in Callicoon. The hamlet grew up around the railroad and was originally called Callicoon Depot, as Callicoon already existed elsewhere (present-day Callicoon Center). Spurred by the railroad, Callicoon Depot quickly outgrew its similarly named neighbor and, to avoid confusion, ultimately became known simply as Callicoon, while the original Callicoon became Callicoon Center. The Western Hotel is shown to the right. *Photo courtesy of Mary Curtis, town of Delaware historian.*

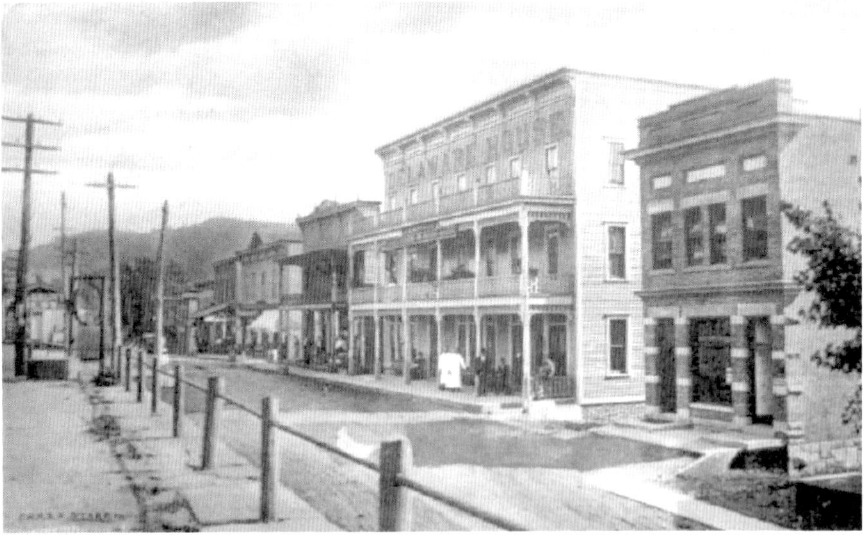

Main Street, Callicoon, showing the Delaware House, a popular hotel in the hamlet. Much of Main Street was destroyed in an 1888 fire, and most of the buildings constructed after that blaze are still stranding. *Photo courtesy of Mary Curtis, town of Delaware historian.*

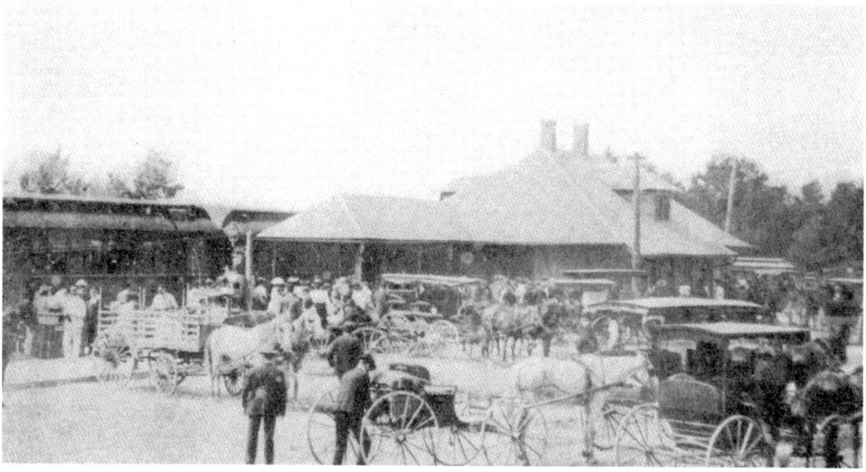

Monticello was spurned twice in its bid for a spot on a mainline railroad, first by the Erie and then by the New York & Oswego Midland. A group of businessmen, led by Thornton A. Niven, C.V.R. Ludington and Giles Benedict, determined that the village should not be without rail service and spearheaded the construction of the Monticello & Port Jervis Railroad in 1871. Monticello's second train station, which is still standing and which has been adaptively reused, is shown.

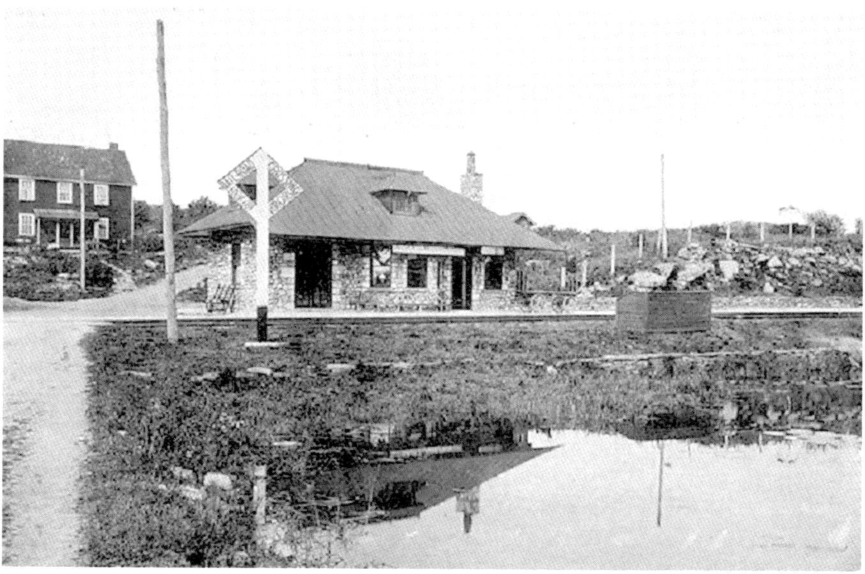

This Monticello & Port Jervis Railroad station at St. Joseph's, formerly Gilmans, was built in 1906 by metals magnate Ambrose Monell, who had purchased much of the property previously owned by W.W. Gilman following the eccentric millionaire's death. The station is made entirely of local river stone and is still standing today.

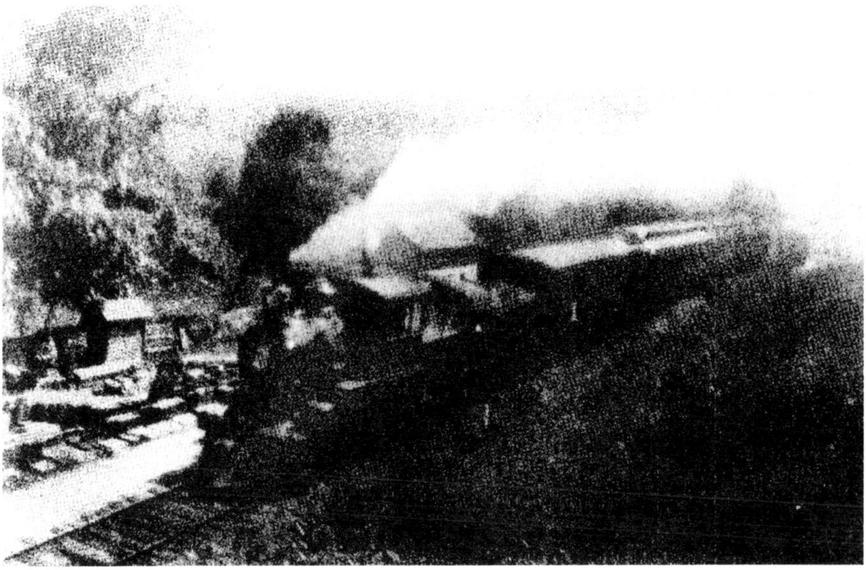

The bluestone industry had a meteoric boom in Sullivan County, reaching its zenith in the 1880s. Here a Monticello & Port Jervis Railroad train carries stone quarried in Oakland Valley in the town of Forestburgh. Quarries were heavily concentrated along the Delaware River but were not exclusive to that area.

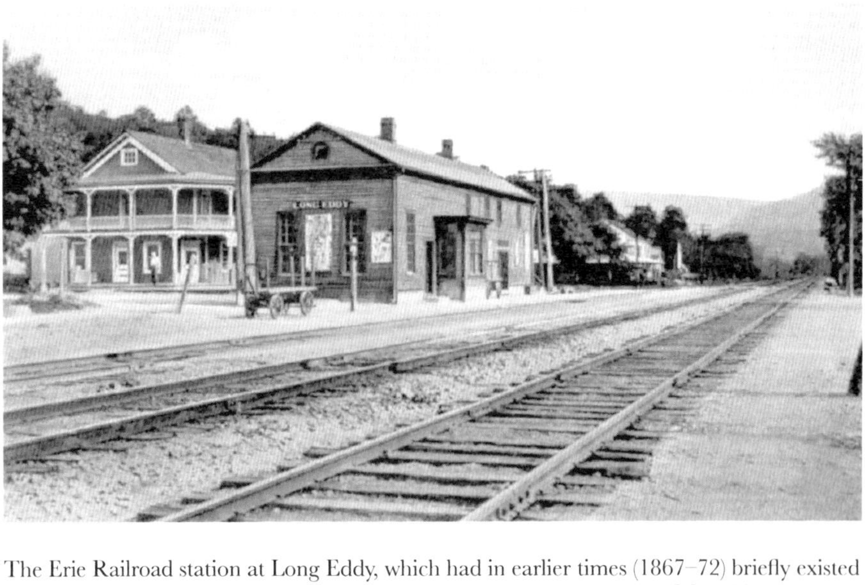

The Erie Railroad station at Long Eddy, which had in earlier times (1867–72) briefly existed as Douglas City, the only incorporated city in Sullivan County's history. More bluestone was quarried in the town of Fremont than anywhere else in the county, and much of it passed through the train station at Long Eddy.

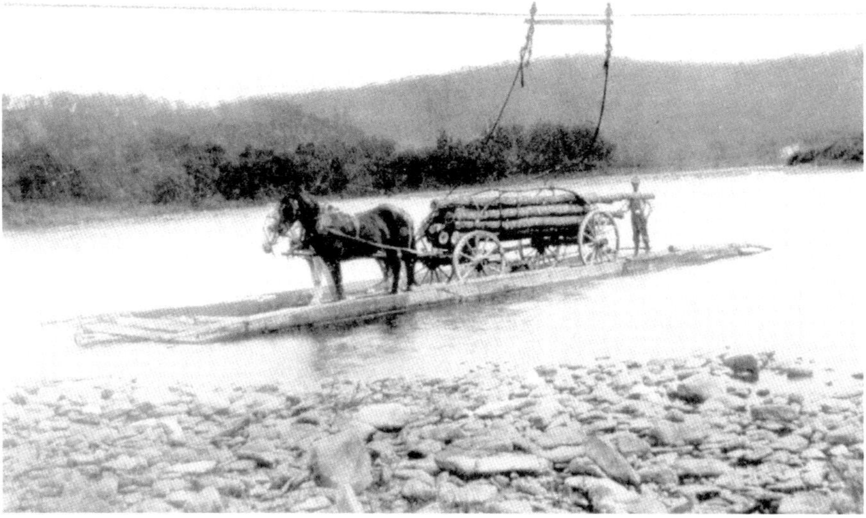

Following the construction of the Erie Railroad tracks along the Pennsylvania side of the Delaware River in 1848, places like Pond Eddy and Barryville, which had not yet constructed bridges across the river, found it necessary to carry freight to the railroad via crude ferry operations. At Barryville, for example, the ferry served as the link to the railroad until the first suspension bridge was built in 1856.

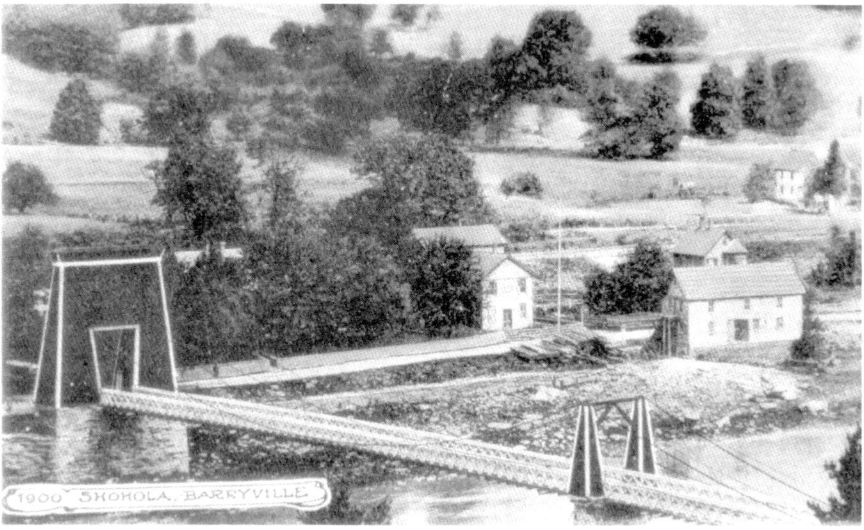

Local contractor Chauncey Thomas built the first Barryville–Shohola suspension bridge in 1856. It was a single span and was not very substantial, requiring replacement in 1859 and again in 1865. A center support was added in 1866, and the bridge served the community until it was replaced by a more modern steel and concrete bridge, built slightly downriver in 1941. That bridge was replaced in 2008.

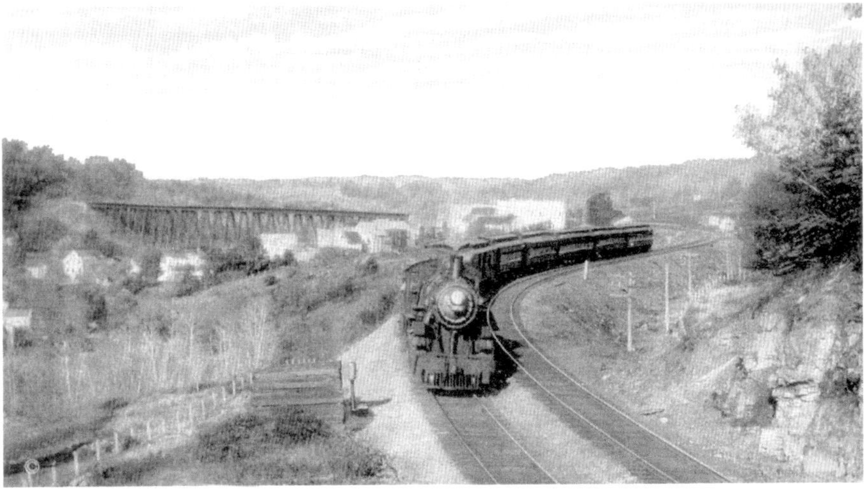

The New York & Oswego Midland Railroad was completed through Sullivan County in the early 1870s but struggled until it became the Ontario & Western (O&W) in the following decade. The O&W was instrumental in opening the county up for tourism, not only by providing passengers with easy access to the mountains, but also by enthusiastically promoting the region as a healing environment.

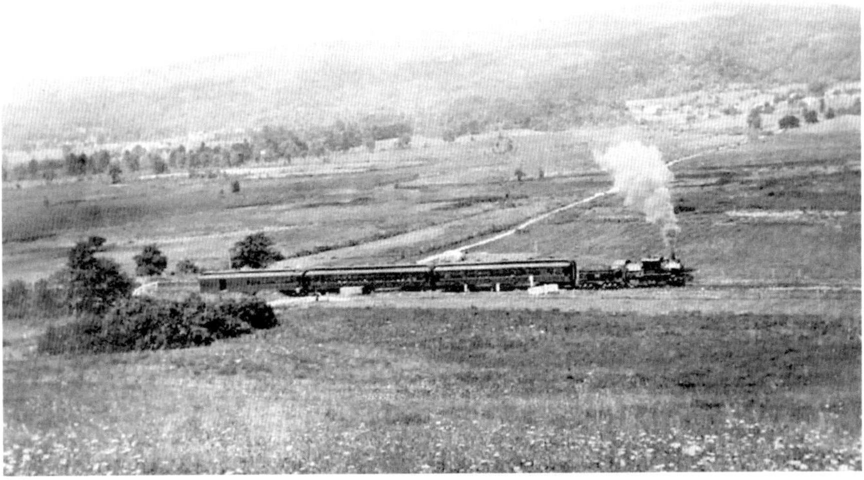

An O&W train speeding through Haven one evening. The tiny Mamakating hamlet was served by the nearby station in High View or Bloomingburgh. Blessed by nature with magnificent views, the Mamakating Valley became a popular tourist destination.

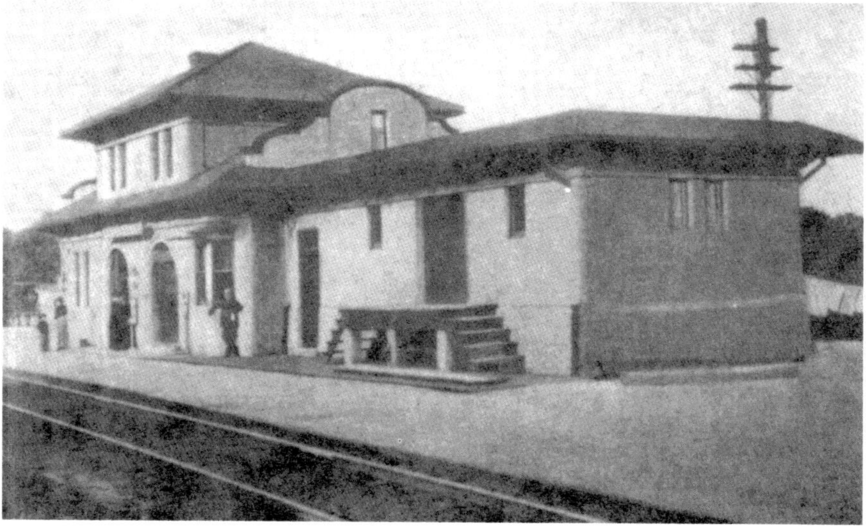

The station at High View served the village of Bloomingburgh, Sullivan County's second-oldest incorporated village (after Monticello), as well as the surrounding area. This photo shows a later High View station, with Sullivan County Mission–style overtones. Note the stucco exterior, the parapet and the arched doorways, which date this photo after 1920.

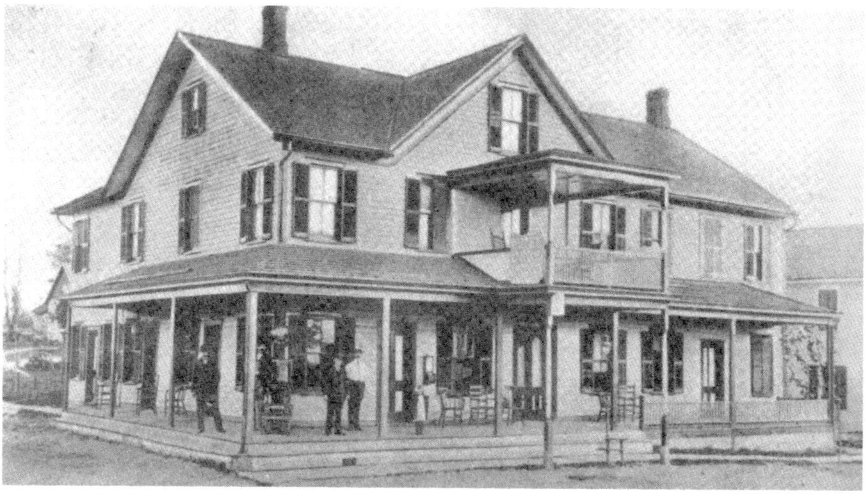

Just as many communities had grown up around the D&H Canal or the local tannery, communities grew up around the railroad too. South Fallsburg is a good example. It didn't even exist when the railroad decided to locate its station about three miles from the industrial hub at Fallsburg (or Old Falls, as it is commonly called today). The railroad at first called the station Mitchell Station, but it quickly became known as South Fallsburg. Pictured is the Hotel LeRoy, which stood just adjacent to the tracks at the corner of Main Street. It was later called the Hotel Ryan.

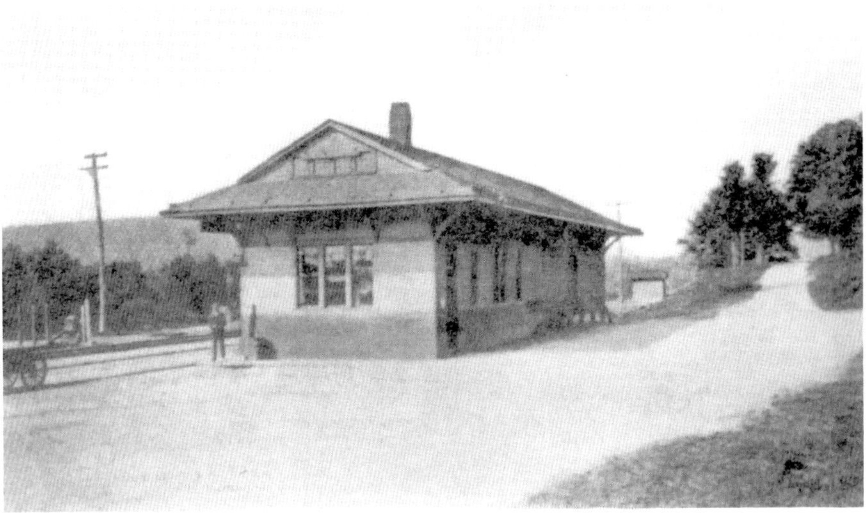

Hurleyville was founded shortly after the dawn of the nineteenth century by an old hunter named William Hurley, who envisioned it as an important settlement. But Hurley miscalculated, and decades later the hamlet consisted of just one house—Hurley's. That all changed when the O&W arrived in the 1870s. To avoid confusion with Hurley in Ulster County, the railroad called the place Luzon Station.

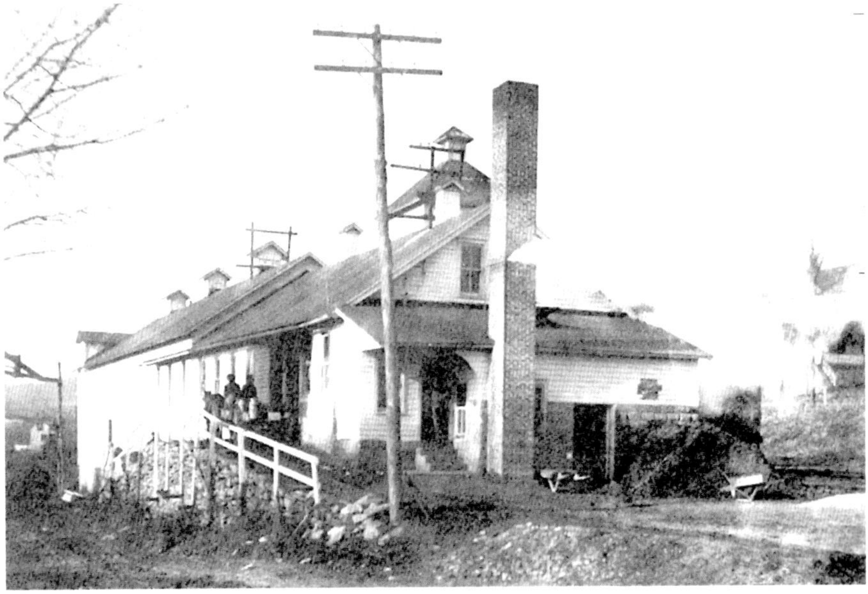

Dairy farmers utilized the railroad to send their milk to market, and the Hurleyville Creamery was among the most modern of several in the county. By 1891, Sullivan County farmers were shipping over seventeen thousand cans of milk to New York. That number steadily increased, and during 1901 nearly nine million cans were shipped.

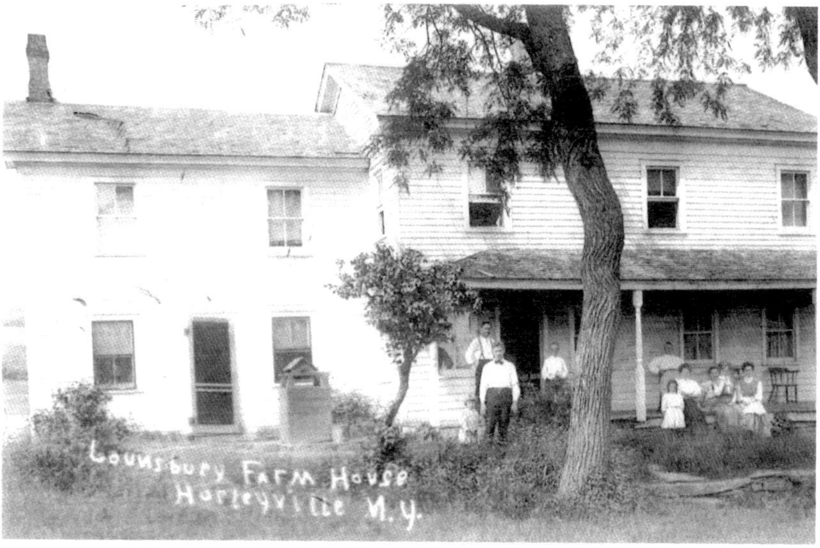

This farmhouse built by Daniel Addison Lounsbury in Hurleyville around 1870 was one of just a half dozen houses in the community before the railroad arrived and the area blossomed. By 1886, the population of Hurleyville had grown to 150, and Lounsbury's was just one of several dairy farms. Daniel Webster Lounsbury took over the farm from his father and cut ice on nearby lakes to supplement the family income during the off season. *Photo courtesy of Paul Lounsbury of Grahamsville.*

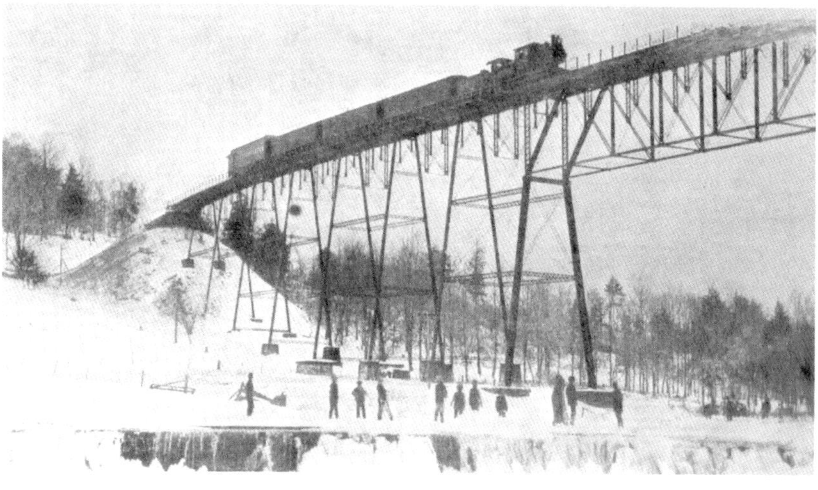

The Ferndale trestle on the O&W Railroad was an engineering marvel. Ferndale had been known as Liberty Falls until resort owners there began fearing the fallout of the stigma Liberty was gaining because of its association with the treatment of tuberculosis. The name Ferndale was borrowed from the area's most popular resort, Joshua Gerow's Ferndale Villa. The area below the trestle was, obviously, a favorite wintertime gathering place.

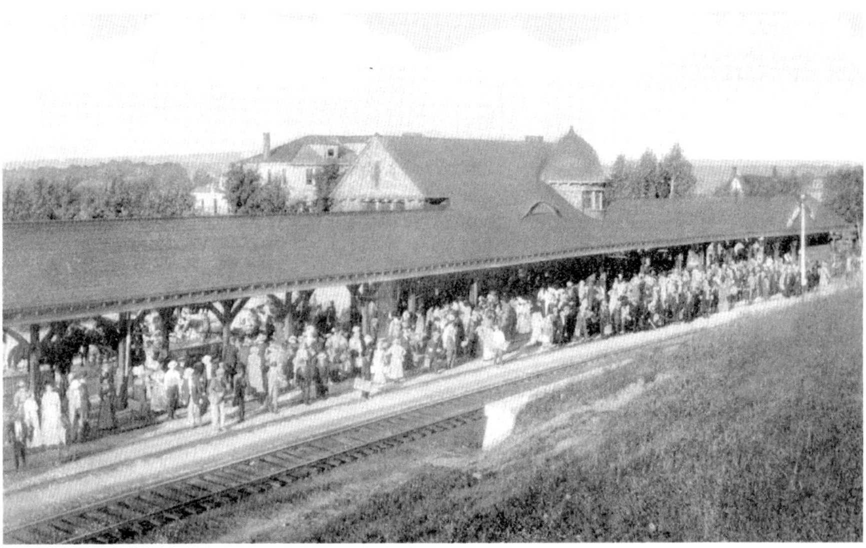

The Liberty Railroad station was one of the area's busiest, serving dozens of hotels in and around the village, as well as those in White Sulphur Springs, Grahamsville and, in some cases, White Lake. This incarnation of the Liberty station was designed by noted railroad architect Bradford Lee Gilbert, himself a part-time Sullivan County resident.

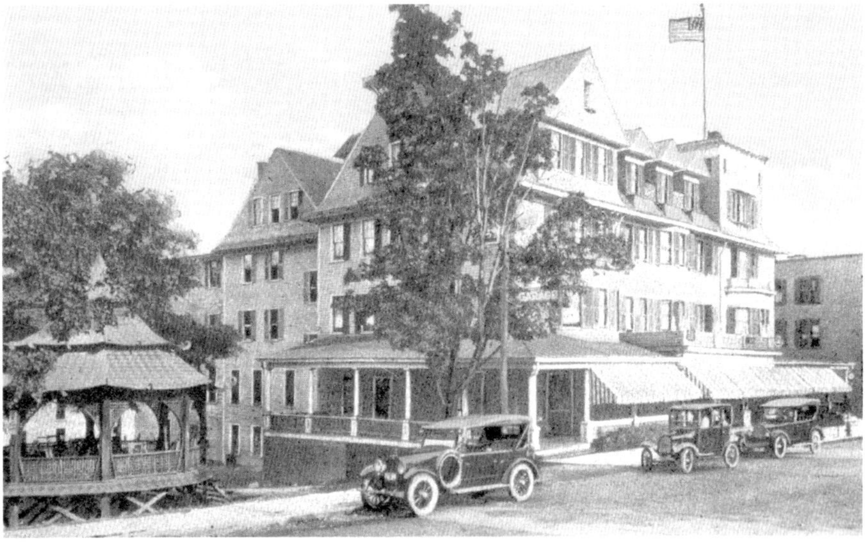

The Liberty House, on the village's Main Street, was one of the county's most famous hotels. Originally built in the 1860s, the hotel served as headquarters for the railroad's surveyors and construction crews. Thomas Houlihan bought the hotel in 1885 and ten years later erected a larger structure (pictured) almost directly across the street. When the Liberty Highway was at the height of its fame, the Liberty House shared in the glory. The hotel burned down in 1926 and was not rebuilt.

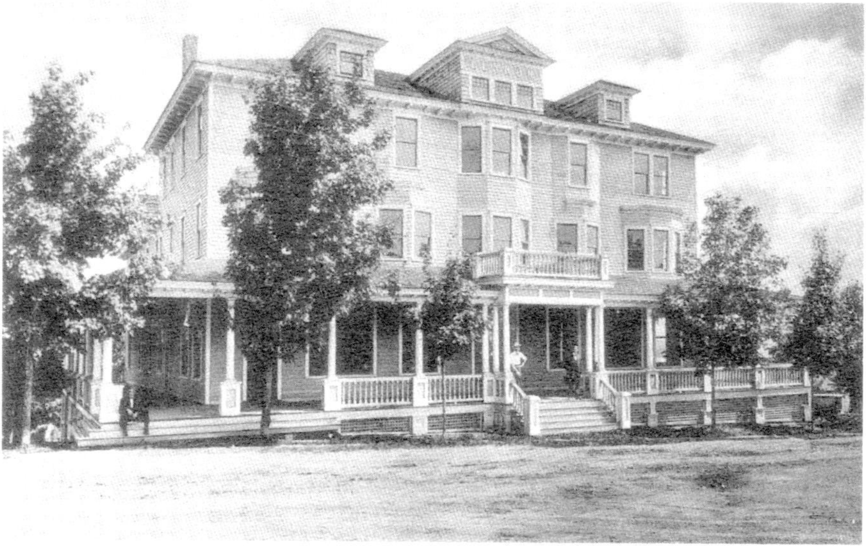

The Lennon House was located adjacent to the railroad station in Liberty and operated under several names. It was fairly typical architecturally of the hotels of the early railroad era.

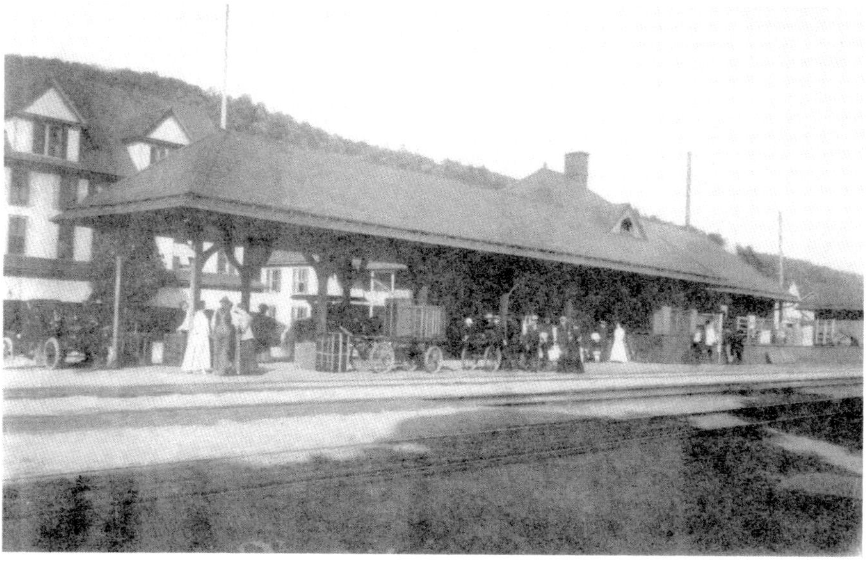

The Roscoe station was the last stop in Sullivan County and served the resort areas of Tennanah Lake, DeBruce, Lew Beach and Beaverkill, as well as the twin hamlets of Roscoe and Rockland. Trout fishing played a major role in the growth of tourism around Roscoe, and the railroad did more than its part to promote the sport, including stocking local streams.

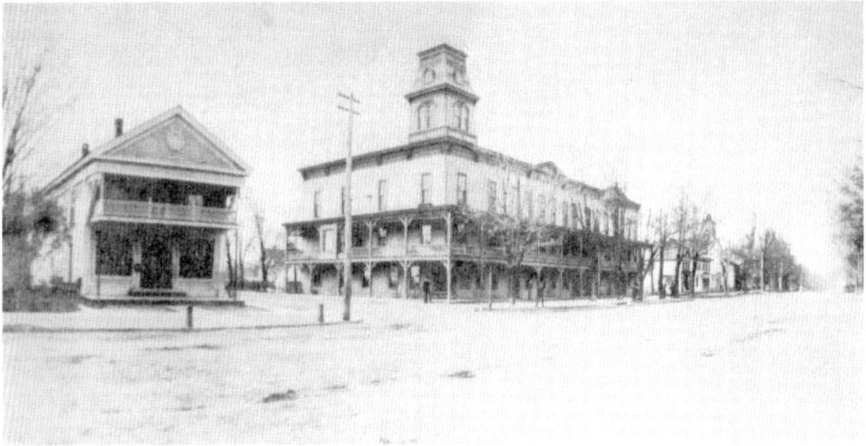

Monticello's famous Hotel Rockwell became popular almost immediately after George Rockwell purchased the Hahn House and renamed it. The smart-looking hotel was located at the southwest corner of Main and Mill Streets (present-day Broadway and St. John), facing the village park and the county courthouse. It was one of the many victims of the 1909 Monticello fire, the most destructive fire in county history. The Monticello post office is shown on the left.

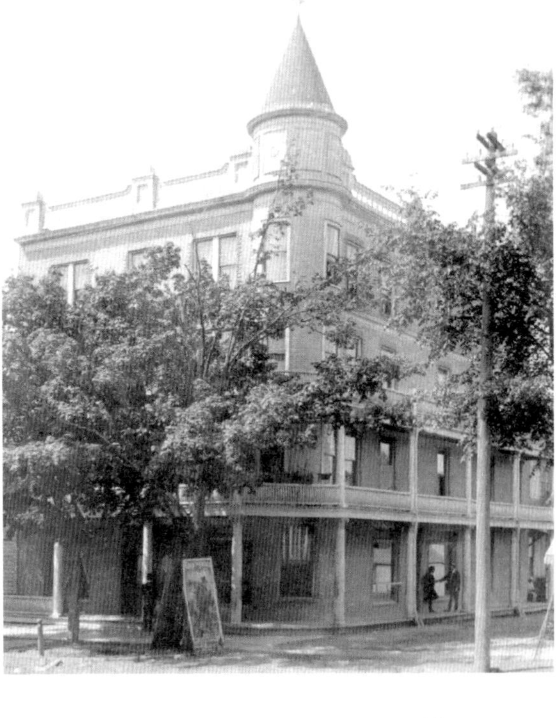

The Palatine Hotel, located on the northwest corner of Main and Orchard Streets (present-day Broadway and Landfield Avenue) in Monticello, was built by Peter C. Murray, who also owned the Palatine Theatre and the power plant that provided electric service not just to his businesses but also to the entire village. The 1909 fire started in the power plant and consumed about half the village's business district, resulting in over $1 million in property losses but no fatalities.

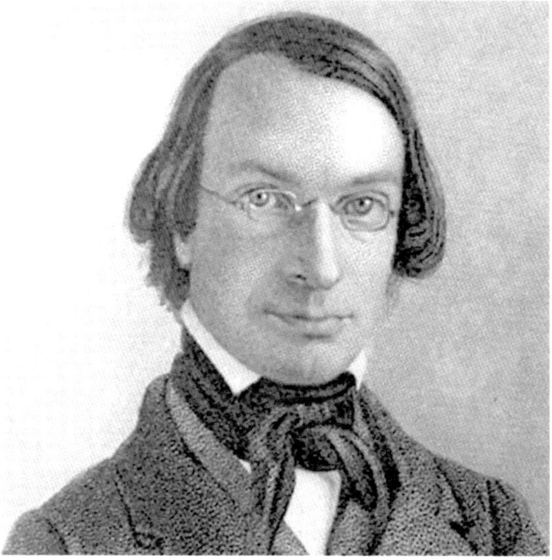

Alfred B. Street was born in Poughkeepsie in 1811 but grew up in Monticello, where he practiced law in his father's law office and wrote poetry describing the incredible natural beauty of the area before the arrival of the tanner and the tourist. Street was an avid fisherman and occasionally wrote for sporting publications as well. His vivid portraits of such natural landmarks as the Mongaup Falls, Kiamesha Lake, the Callicoon Creek and the Willowemoc helped lure tourists to the county. Street died in 1881.

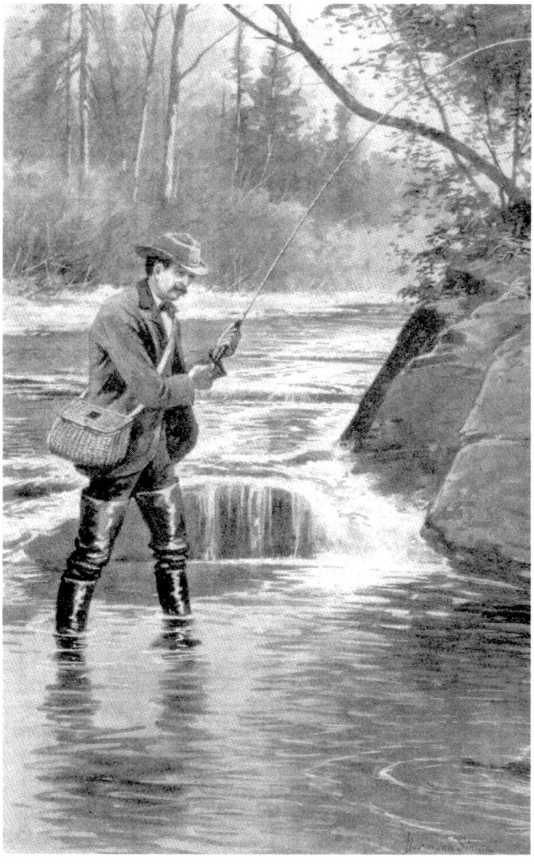

The Beaverkill has long been one of the most famous trout streams in all of America and was often featured in sporting publications. The legendary stream's bounty has never been surpassed, though the Willowemoc, the Callicoon and the Mongaup Creek have all enjoyed nearly equal standing at times. Trout fishing played an enormous role in the early development of tourism in the county.

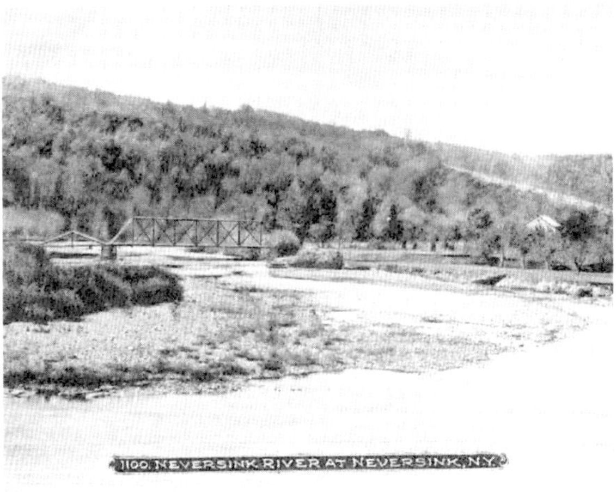

The Neversink River has at times been revered by fishermen, particularly those who prize solitude and pristine shorelines. One of the principal sources of water power in the industrial days of the county, and one of the few waterways never utilized for timber rafting (several attempts failed miserably), the river became an important tourist destination when the county made the transition to a resort economy. *Photo courtesy of Time and the Valleys Museum, Grahamsville.*

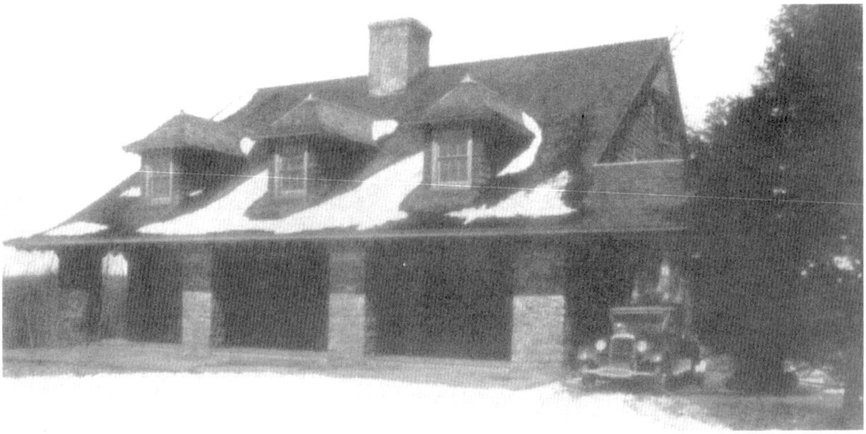

Millionaire industrialist Chester W. Chapin's Elk Lodge served as his rustic but state-of-the-art home in Sullivan County. Chapin, noted yachtsman and a crack shot, kept white-tailed deer, elk and dozens of different types of small game on his twenty-thousand-acre preserve, where he hunted and fished in the company of contemporaries Thomas Edison, Louis Comfort Tiffany and Bradford Lee Gilbert, among others.

Chapter 3

THE SILVER AGE

By the time the 1890s rolled around, Sullivan County had entered into a period of tourism-based prosperity that historians today call the Silver Age. The hotels that populated the region during this period were largely served by the railroad, so most—though by no means all—were located within walking distance of the stations. They were offering their guests a relaxing stay in the country, so lakes and streams were important as well. In fact, as the area made its transition from timber and tanning to tourism, many of the ponds in the area, which had served the tanneries and mills, became lakes overnight. The picturesque replaced the perfunctory in the names of these bodies of water. Pike Pond, for example, became Kenoza Lake; Long Pond became Tennanah Lake; Pleasant Pond became Kiamesha Lake; Hagan's Pond was renamed Highland Lake; and so on.

Silver Age hotels were typically Victorian wood-frame structures with steeply pitched roofs and multiple porches. Most were a single building, though some eventually added an annex. Most were open only in the summer. And, most were gentile owned. In fact, prior to 1899, there was no mention at all of Jewish hotels or vacationers in the area that would become known for its Jewish hotels and vacationers.

John Gerson became the first Jewish resort owner to advertise his business in 1899. Gerson, whose small boardinghouse was located in Rock Hill, later built the New Prospect Hotel, which became the Hotel Levitt in Fallsburg.

During this period of prosperity, wealthy sportsmen also began to discover Sullivan County. George Ross Mackenzie, the Scottish-born president of the Singer Sewing Machine Company, had settled in South Lebanon years before and renamed it Glen Spey. Mackenzie built a castellated mansion that he called the Homestead for himself in the 1880s and added a golf course (he was Scottish born, after all!) in 1895. He would eventually build mansions for each of his children, a practice the family continued after his death.

Industrialist Chester W. Chapin, an avid sportsman, accumulated over twenty thousand acres and created his own game preserve. His guests included Thomas Edison, Louis Comfort Tiffany and Bradford Lee Gilbert. William Howe Crane, a judge in nearby Port Jervis, started the Hartwood Club for his wealthy sportsman friends in Forestburgh, and his brother, the writer Stephen Crane, became a frequent guest, eventually living there at the home of another brother, Edmund.

By about 1915, the Silver Age had come to an end, partly because of the growing reputation that the county was gaining as a haven for tuberculosis patients. The Loomis Sanitarium outside Liberty had become one of the most renowned treatment centers in America, and dozens of other facilities were soon in operation. Some of these smaller facilities even hung the patients' dirty laundry out their windows. Resort owners were indignant. Healthy vacationers were wary of spending time surrounded by "consumptives," and the tourism industry suffered greatly. Before long, yet another transition was underway.

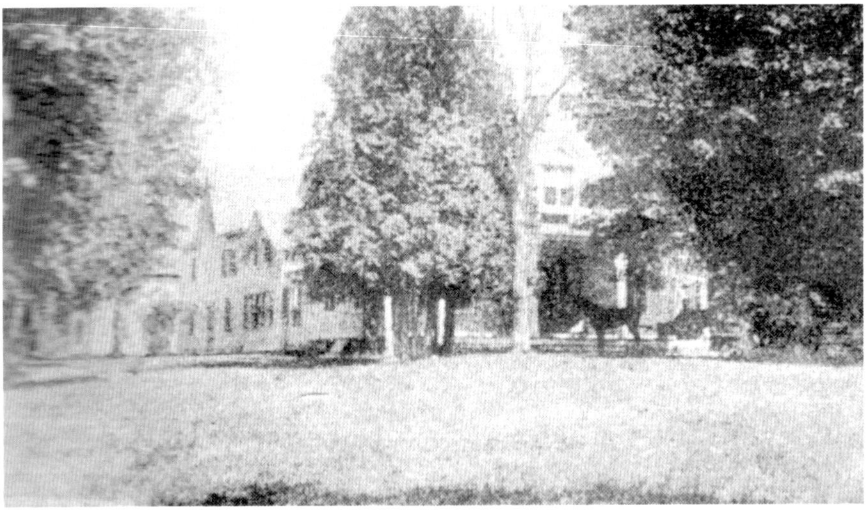

The Flagler House was built on the Neversink River in Fallsburg by tanner Nicholas Flagler in 1872 and was operated by his daughter, Carrie Flagler Angel. By 1902, it had expanded to include accommodations for seventy and offered its guests lawn tennis and croquet. One of the area's pioneering summer resorts, it would later play a significant role in the evolution of tourism in the county.

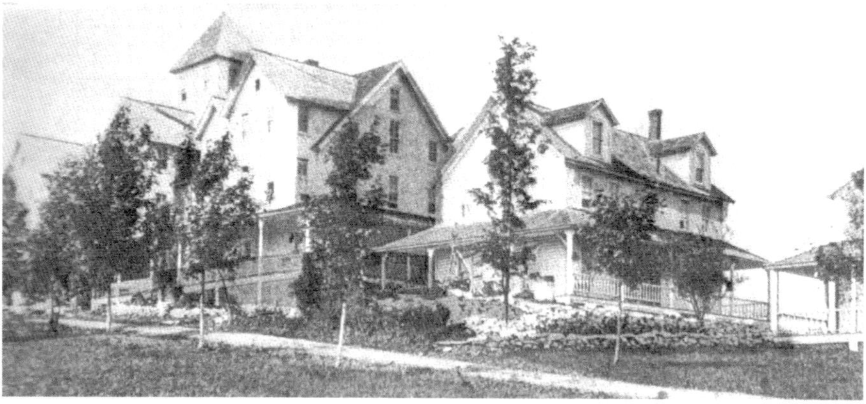

Lakewood Farms, which overlooked Lake Florence near Roscoe, was originally built in 1887. The hotel burned down in 1897 and was immediately rebuilt, bigger and better than ever. John D. Rockefeller stayed there each summer for many years before the hotel met its final demise by fire in 1932. The resort featured one of the earliest golf courses in the county, constructed just after 1900.

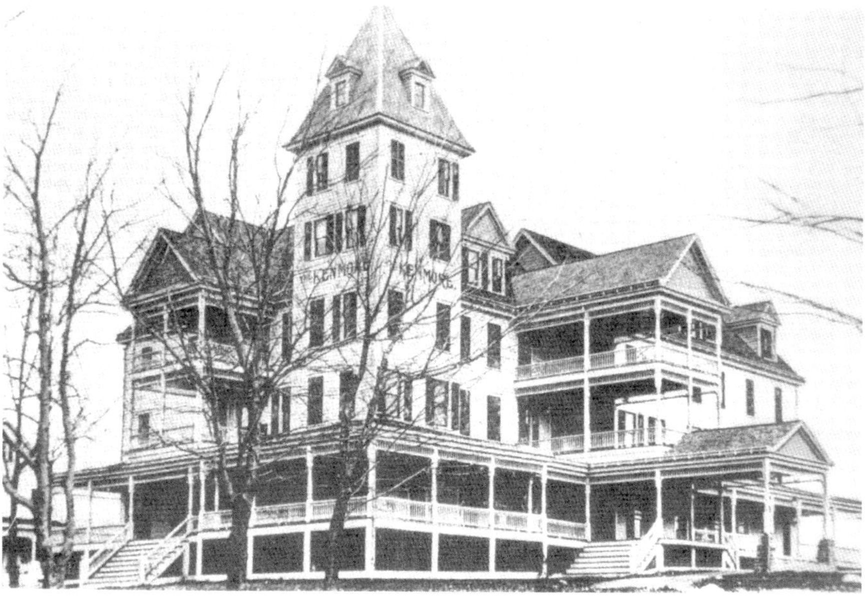

White Lake's Kenmore Hotel was typical of the county's Silver Age resorts in that it was located adjacent to a body of water (in this case, the lake) and featured multiple porches and a distinctive corner tower. Sadly, this version of the Kenmore burned down in 1947. It was rebuilt as a modern structure, but without the Victorian flair.

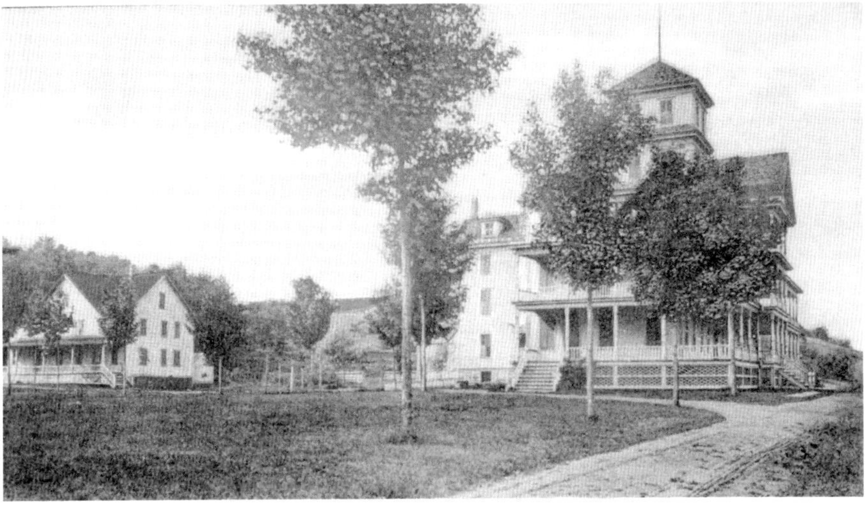

The Columbia Farms Hotel in Hurleyville was known as "Knapp's Folly" when it was first built by John Harms Knapp in 1891. It quickly became one of the area's leading Christian resorts and was the county's oldest continuously operating (same ownership) resort when it closed in 1969. The main house, shown here, is of typical Victorian architecture, with multiple porches and a tower similar to the Kenmore's. An annex is shown nearby.

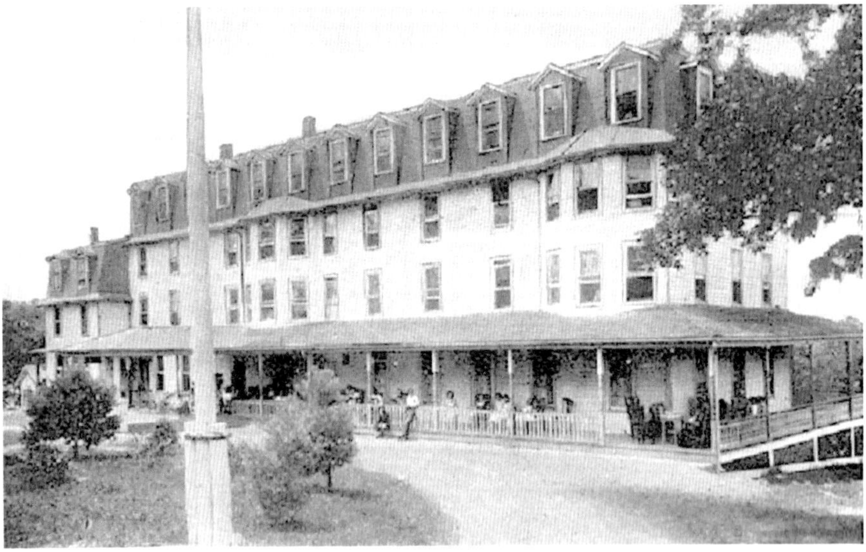

The upper Delaware Valley developed as a tourist destination before the rest of Sullivan County, and many of the early resorts remained unchanged until their demise. The Highland Lake Inn was one of the larger and more popular hotels on the picturesque lake that featured many lively places to stay.

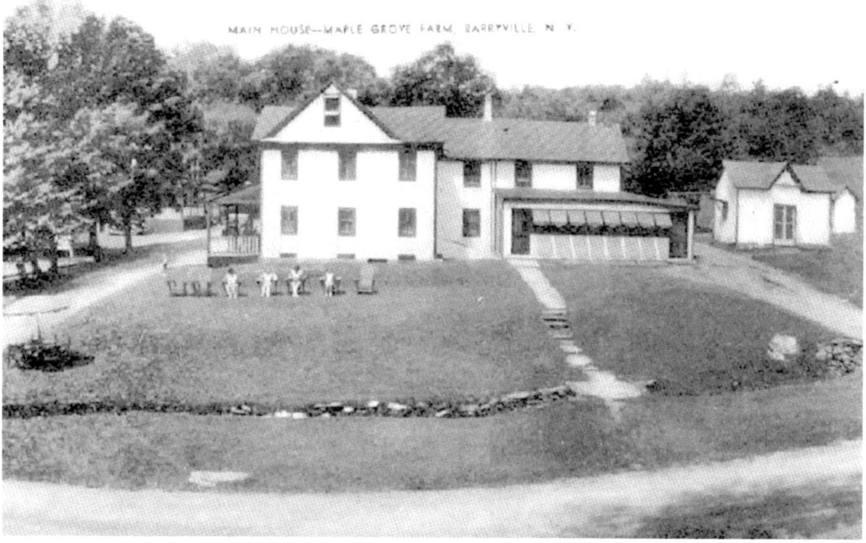

The Maple Grove in Barryville was typical of many upper Delaware Valley resorts. In later years, it was not uncommon to see slot machines and other gambling devices at some of these small hotels.

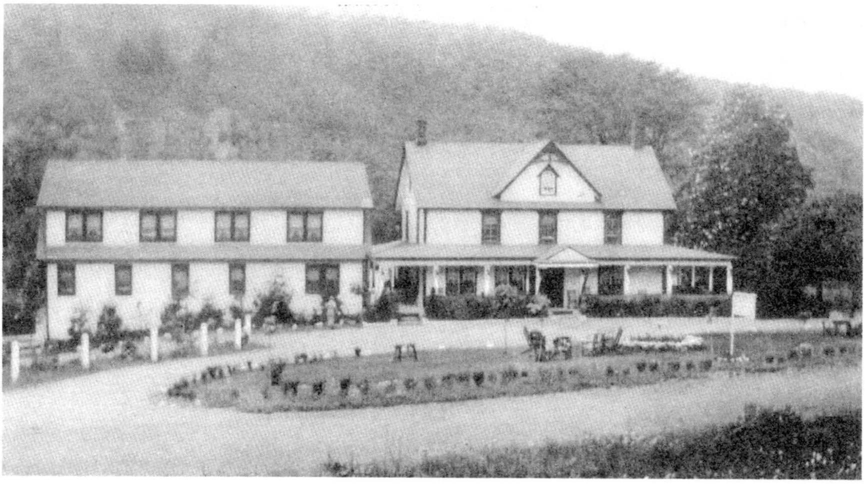

Handsome Eddy Farm, just downriver from Barryville, featured riverfront property accessing an eddy—what the locals call a section of the river where the current turns slowly back on itself, creating, in effect, a very slow whirlpool that results in a pond-like surface conducive to swimming and leisurely boating, unlike the more active sections of the river.

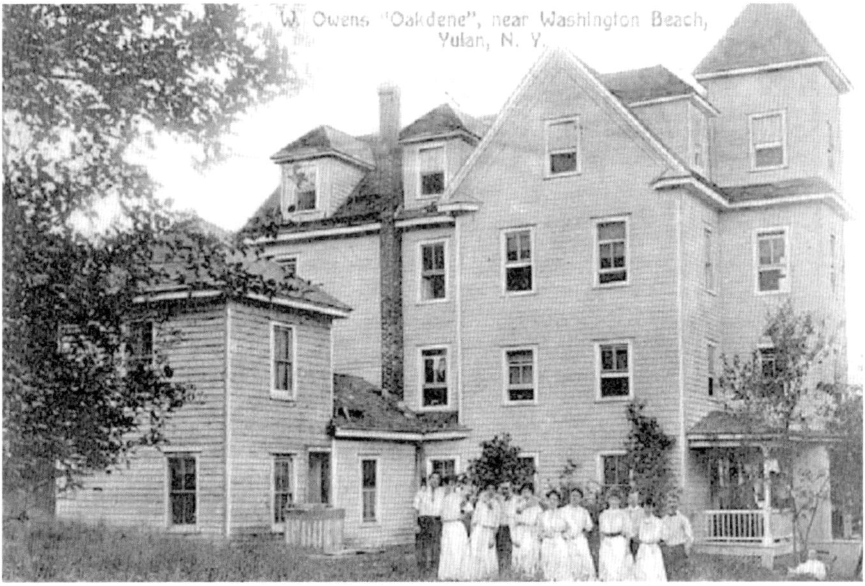

Oakdene, in Yulan, another small resort in the upper Delaware Valley, was one of several that were especially convenient to the beaches of Washington Lake.

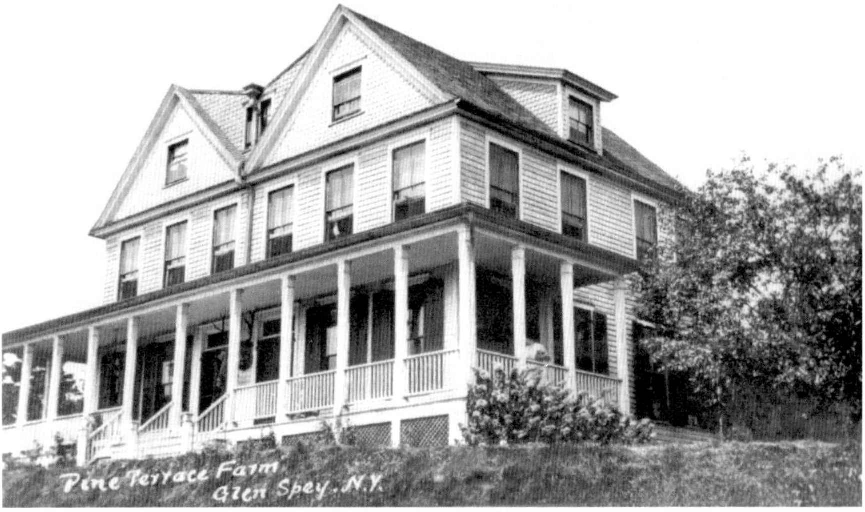

Franz August Schwarz, noted violinist, retired to Glen Spey around 1910 to operate the tidy Pine Terrace Boarding House. *Photo courtesy of Frank V. Schwarz, town of Lumberland historian, and the Glen Spey Museum.*

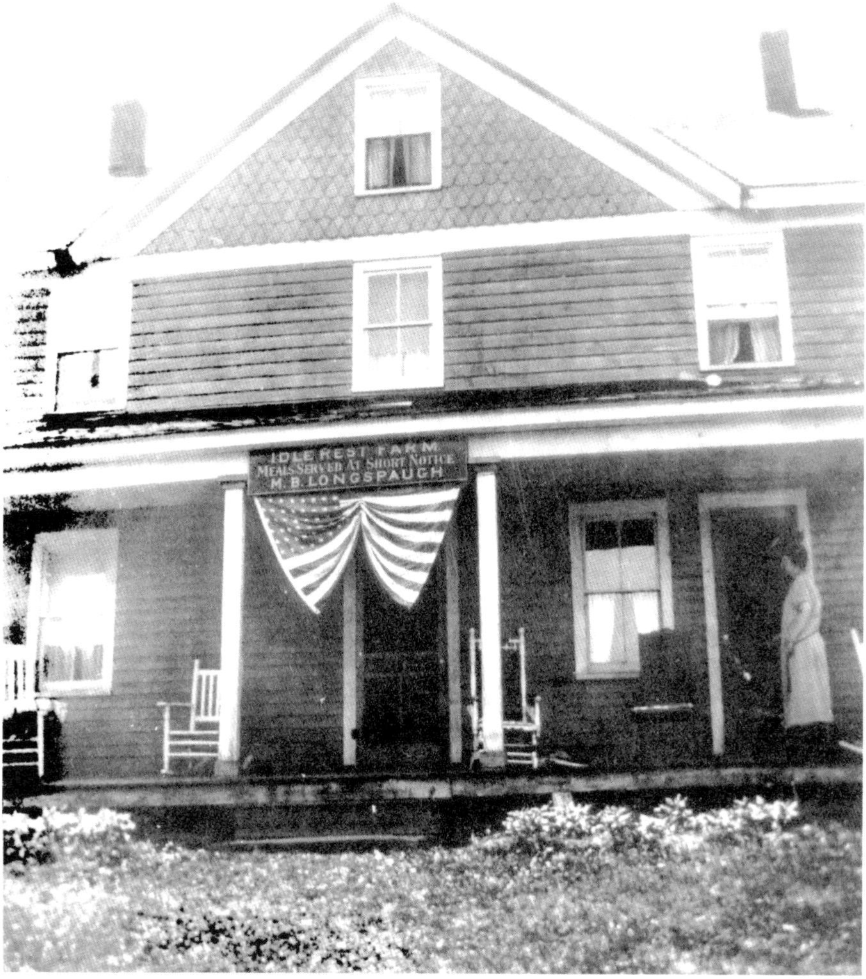

The Longspaugh Boarding House in Upper Mongaup offered guests just a few rooms but easy access to the recreational opportunities of the upper Delaware region. *Photo courtesy of Frank V. Schwarz, town of Lumberland historian, and the Glen Spey Museum.*

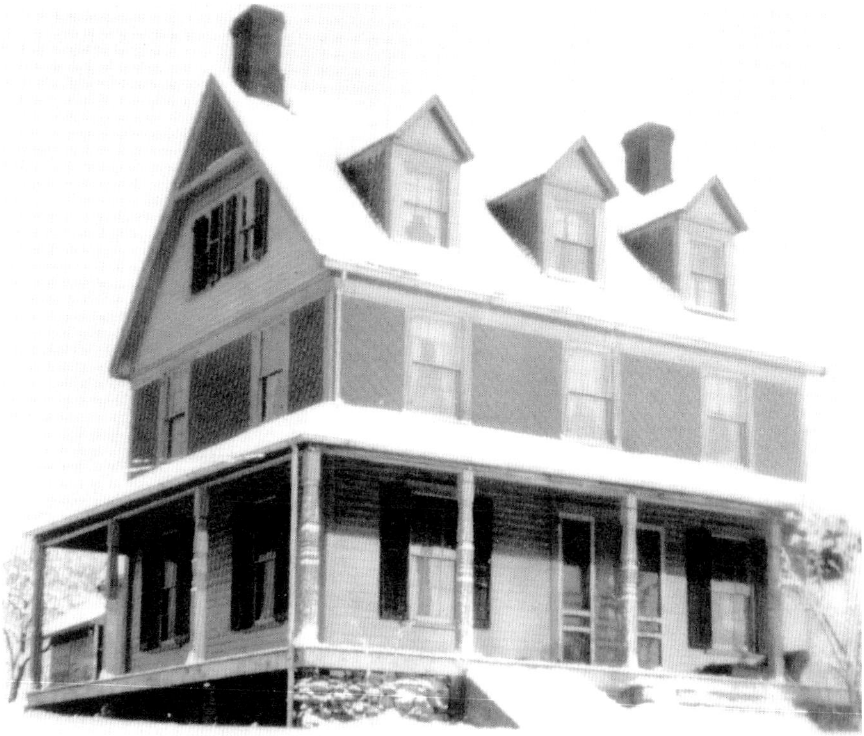

The Brandt Boardinghouse in the town of Lumberland. *Photo courtesy of Frank V. Schwarz, town of Lumberland historian, and the Glen Spey Museum.*

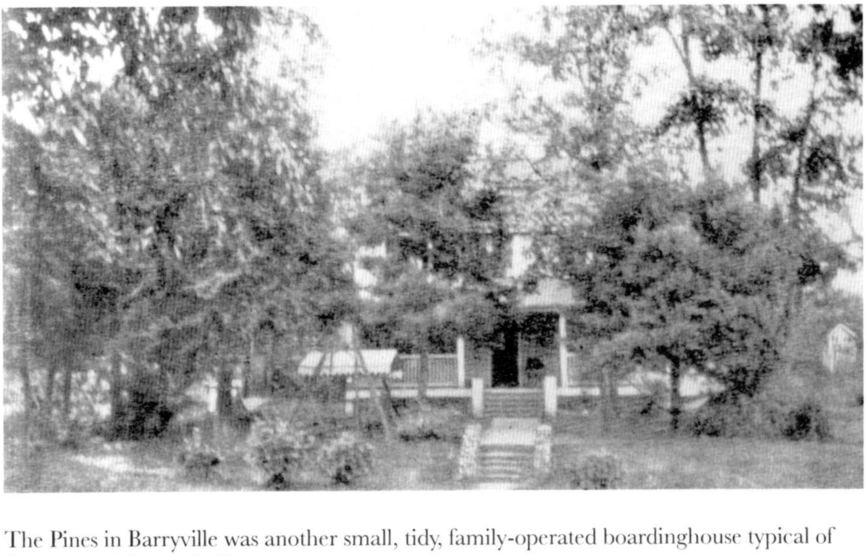

The Pines in Barryville was another small, tidy, family-operated boardinghouse typical of the upper Delaware Valley.

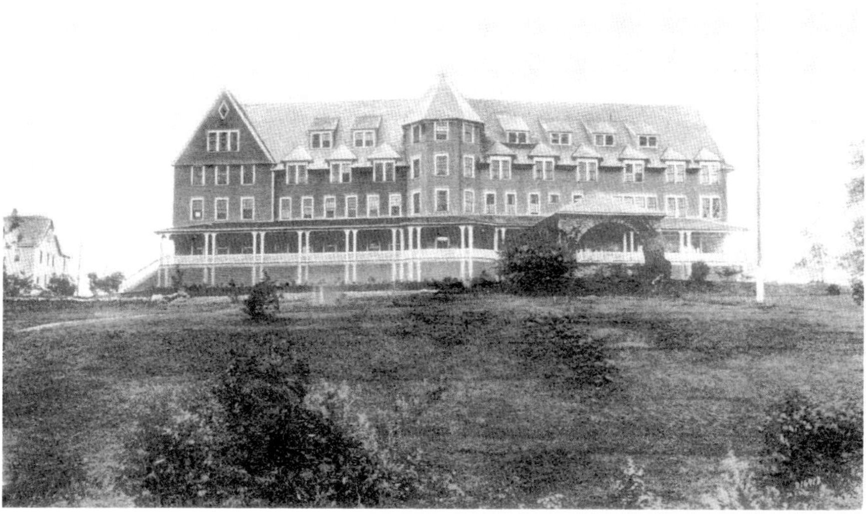

Ye Lancashire Inn, one of Liberty's premier resorts, was built in 1893. It was a favorite with Cuban visitors and hosted Caesar Romero when he was a young boy. It also counted Pierre Lorillard of tobacco fame among its regular guests. The hotel burned down long after its heyday in 1920, having outlasted many of its contemporaries.

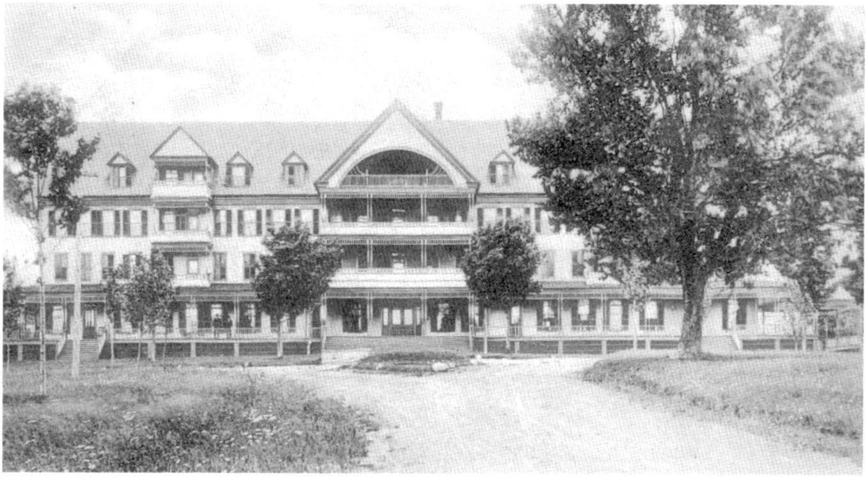

The Hotel Wawonda in Liberty was the county's largest and most elaborate Silver Age resort. Built in 1891, the hotel eventually boasted tennis courts, a golf course and a two-mile-long bicycle track, along with more than three hundred rooms. The Wawonda had a whirlwind existence, and by 1910 it had fallen on hard times, a victim of the Liberty area's association with tuberculosis. It burned down in 1914.

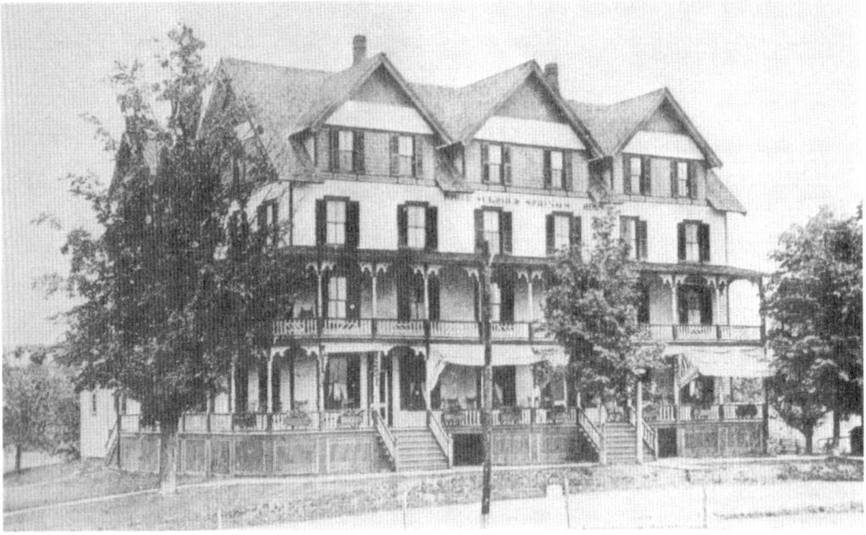

Henry Ernhout's White Sulphur Springs House was significant not only because it lent its name to the erstwhile community of Robertsonville, but also because it became the first hotel in Sullivan County to advertise a medicinal spring located nearby. Thousands flocked to take to the waters, which were claimed to have the same chemical content as the famed baths at San Moritz.

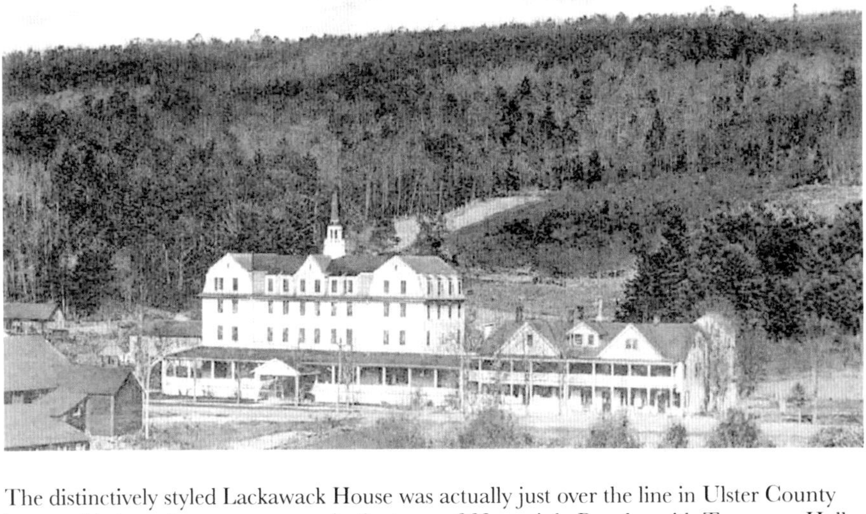

The distinctively styled Lackawack House was actually just over the line in Ulster County but provided employment to many in the town of Neversink. Popular with Tammany Hall politicians seeking refuge from the literal and figurative heat of the city, the hotel burned down in 1917.

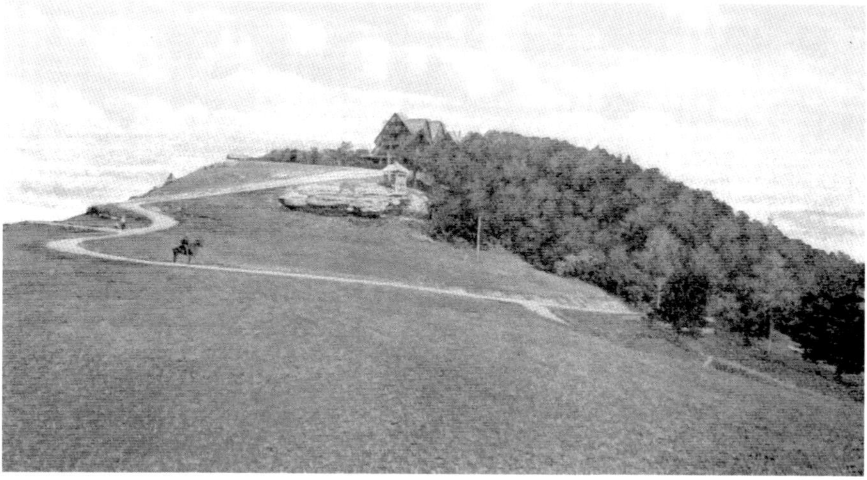

Another prominent Liberty-area Silver Age resort, the Walnut Mountain House was located on one of the highest points in the county and featured breathtaking views of the surrounding area. It was built by W.B. Holmes and opened in 1887.

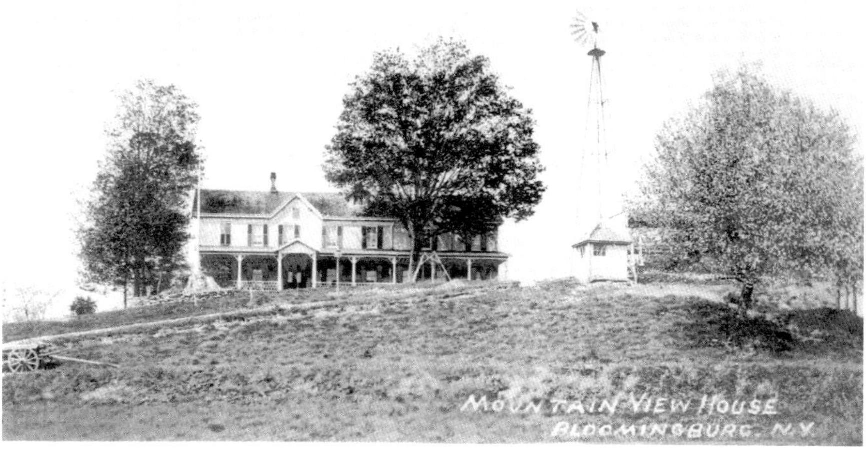

Bloomingburg's Mountain View House was aptly named, offering guests panoramic views of the Mamakating Valley from its perch up on the Shawangunk range.

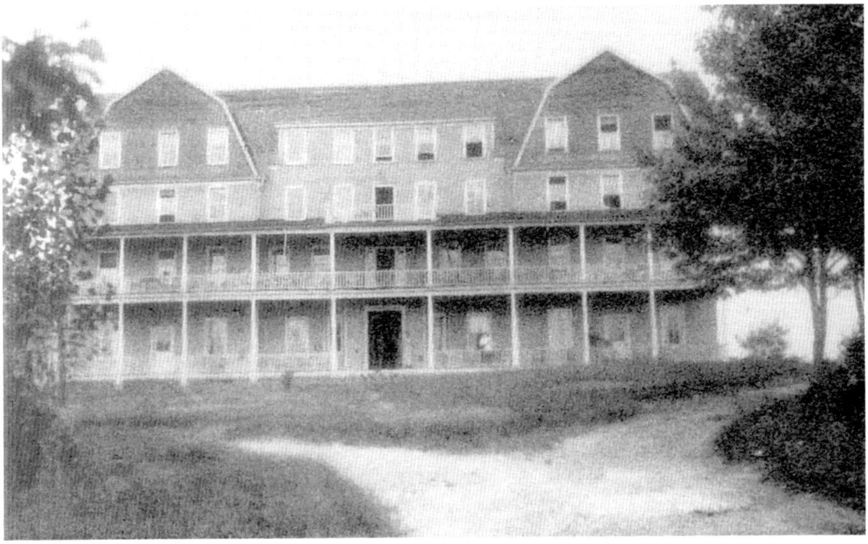

The Hoffman House, one of dozens of small resorts in White Lake, was a simple boardinghouse offering guests an unimpeded vantage point of the lake.

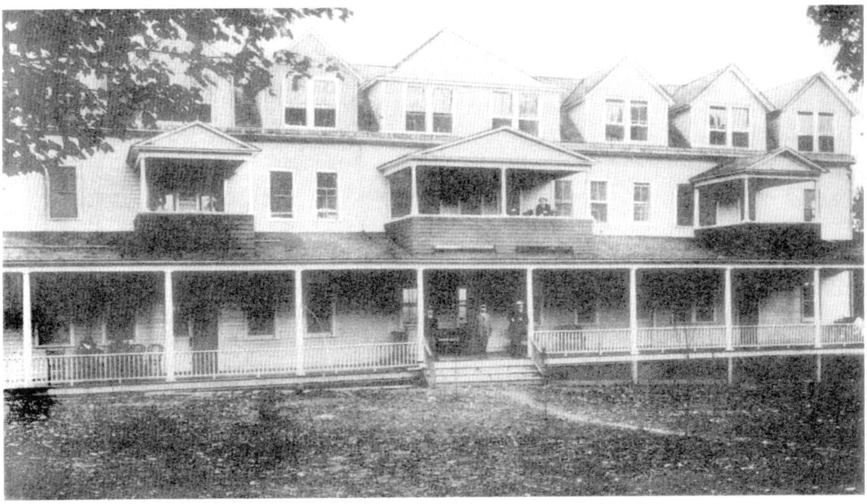

The Morningside in Fallsburg started out as a simple Silver Age hotel but evolved into a prominent resort of the Golden Age, a favorite with the Jewish gangsters who frequented the area in the 1920s and '30s.

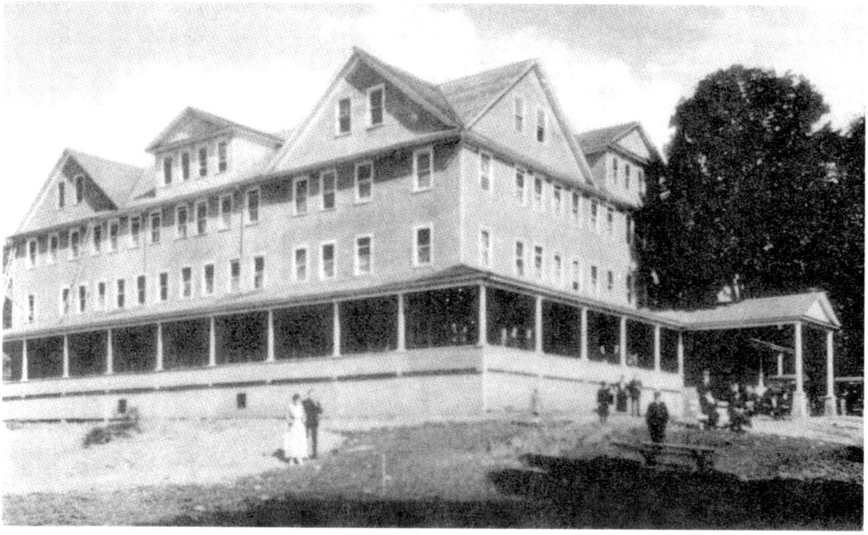

The Hotel Glass, located diagonally across the street from the famed Flagler, started out looking like this but evolved over the years into a classic Golden Age resort. It was later known as the Saxony and, still later, as the Polonia.

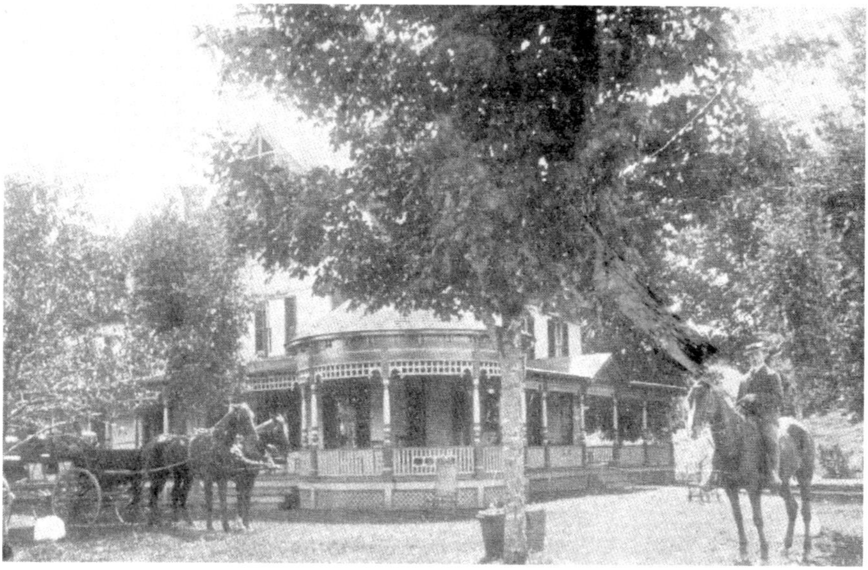

Trout Valley Farm, located on the Beaverkill, offered guests access to unparalleled trout fishing and the area's first golf course, built in 1897. Among the early regulars at the resort was fisherman and fly tier Theodore Gordon.

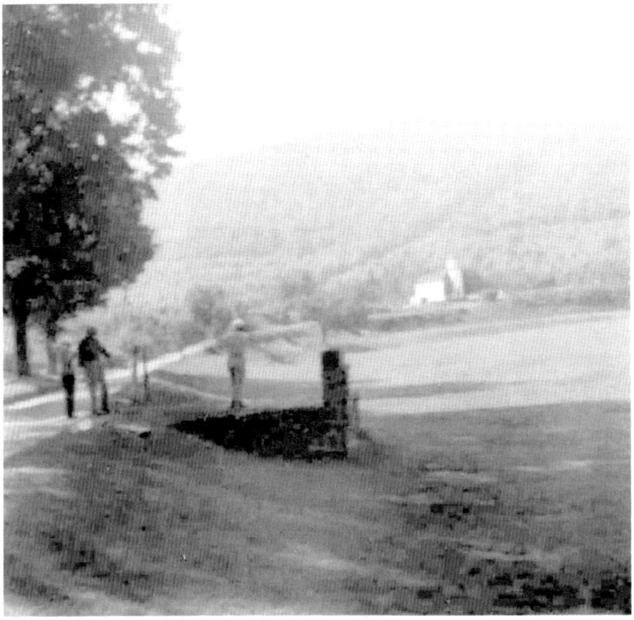

The nine-hole, par-thirty-one Trout Valley Farm golf course was built from a sheep pasture and for a time utilized sheep to keep the grass on the fairways short. This photo shows golfers on the first tee, with the Beaverkill Church in the far distance. The course operated into the 1960s, when the property was purchased by New York State and was allowed to grow back. *Photo courtesy of the Friends of the Beaverkill.*

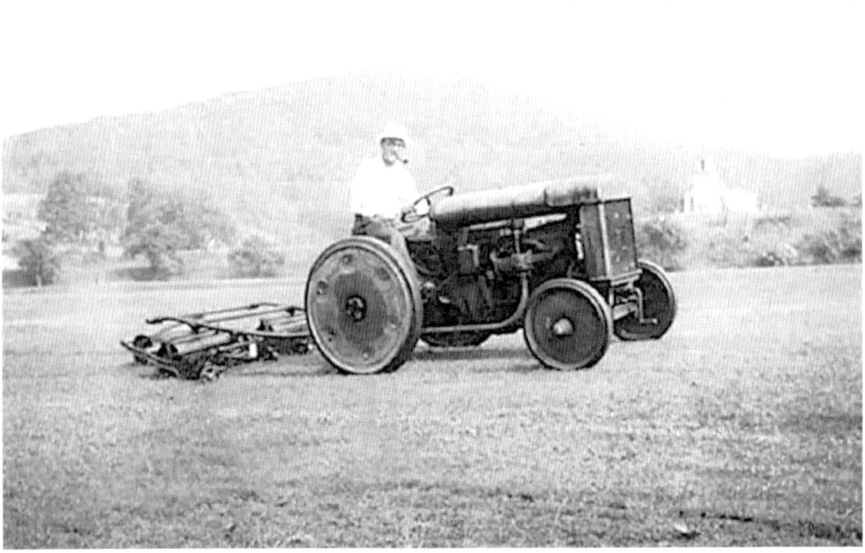

Hotel owner Fred Banks mowing the Trout Valley Farm golf course in later years. Guests at Trout Valley Farm regularly competed in trout fishing and golfing competitions, as well as in baseball games with guests from neighboring hotels. *Photo courtesy of the Friends of the Beaverkill.*

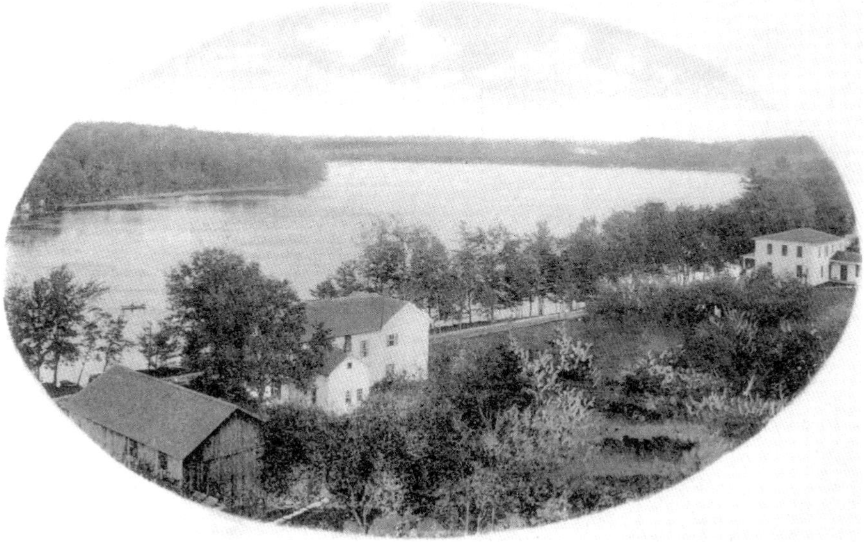

Lake Huntington developed as a tourist destination despite the fact that it was well off the beaten track. Its tranquil and serene beauty drew vacationers back year after year.

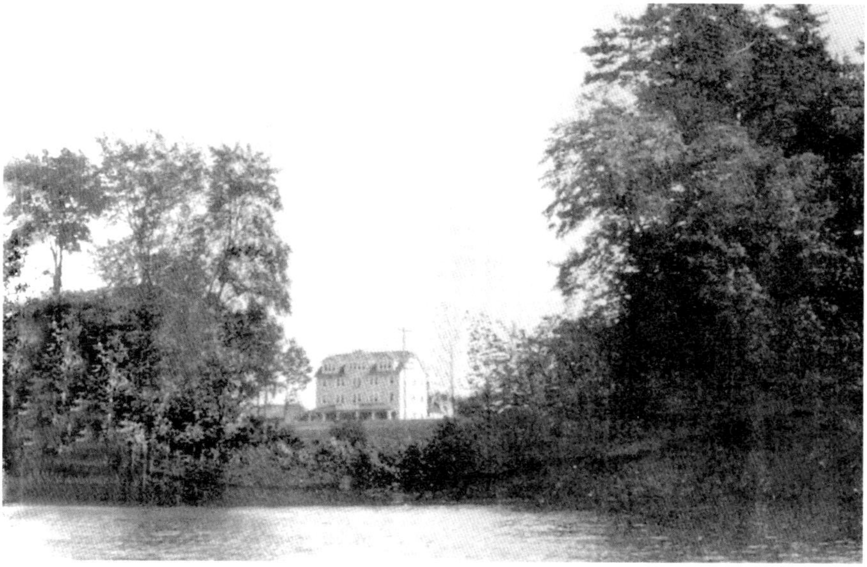

The Pine Grove, overlooking the picturesque lake, was one of the pioneer resorts in Lake Huntington.

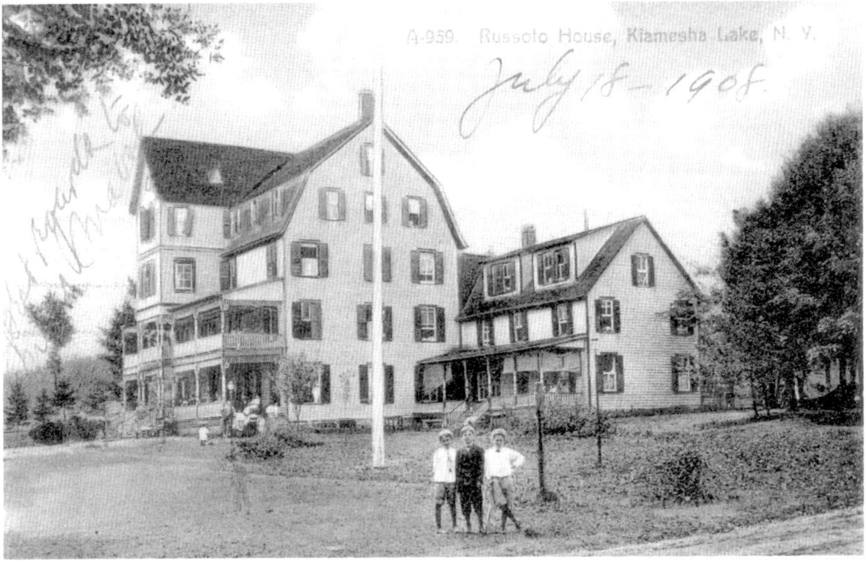

Kiamesha Lake became a prominent tourist destination served by both the Monticello stop on the Monticello & Port Jervis Railroad and the South Fallsburg station on the O&W. The lake was the main attraction, as guests at the Russoto House (pictured) well knew. There were dozens of other hotels and boardinghouses in the late nineteenth and early twentieth centuries, including the Kiamesha Inn, Conway's and Trowbridge's, as well as the famous Bonnie golf links.

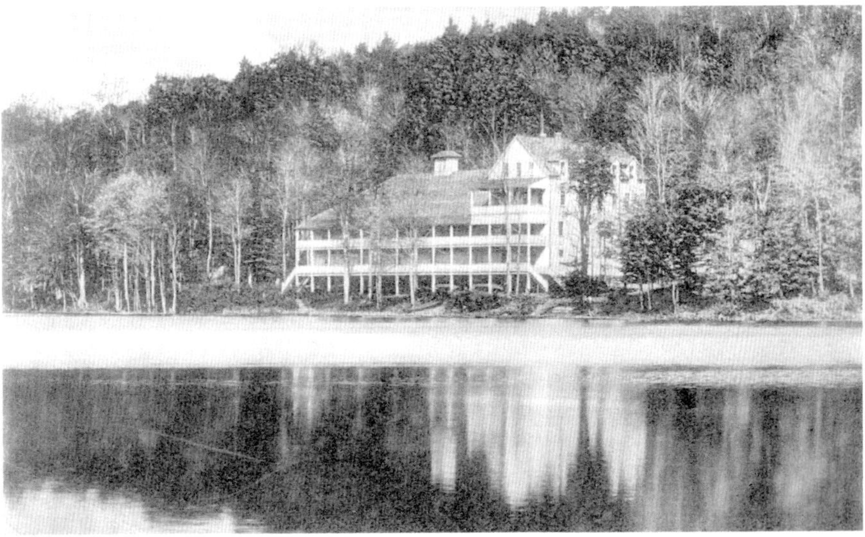

The pavilion at Liberty's Lake Ophelia provided access to one of the county's shallowest lakes, but one that featured boating and bathing in the summer and skating in the winter. Because it was so shallow, Lake Ophelia was often polluted and was eventually drained. Route 17, the Quickway, was constructed over the dry lake bed.

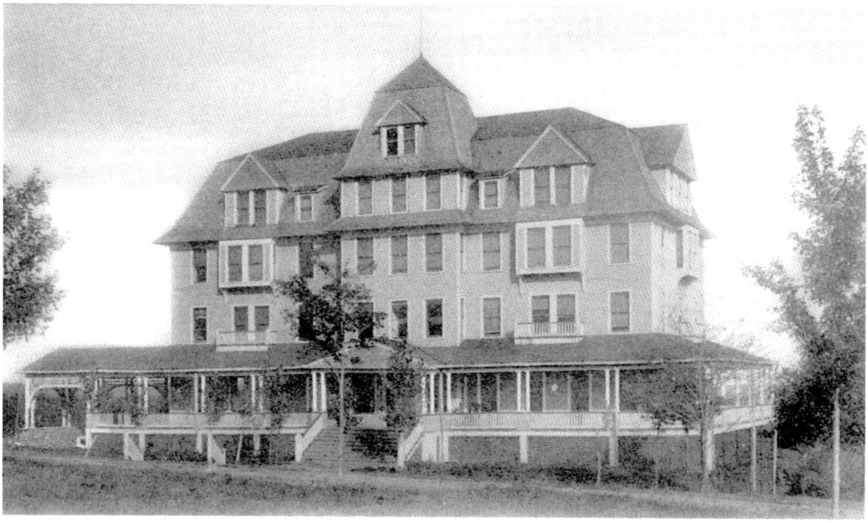

The Monitor was another of Liberty's many Silver Age hotels. Overlooking the village, it offered guests the typical amenities of the era: fresh air, clean water and plenty of shade.

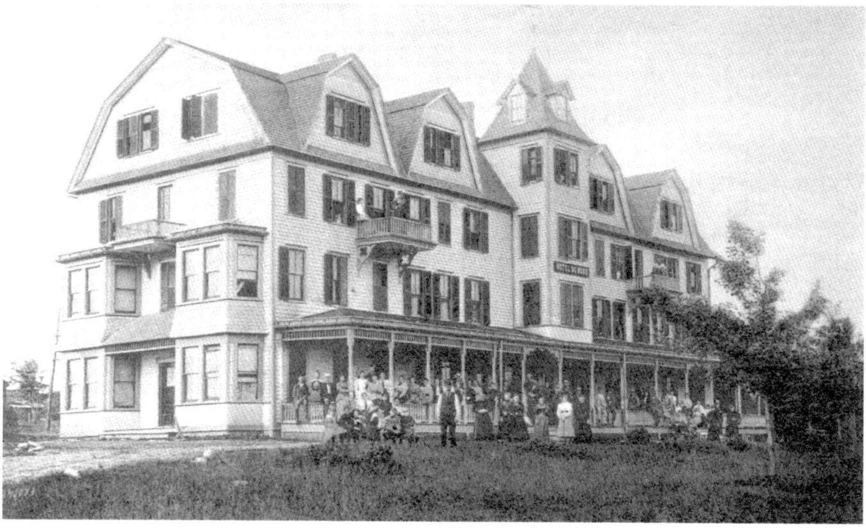

Liberty's Hotel DuNord, owned by the Dohrman family, was an architectural hodgepodge that, legend has it, was later sawed in half because of a disagreement between two of its owners.

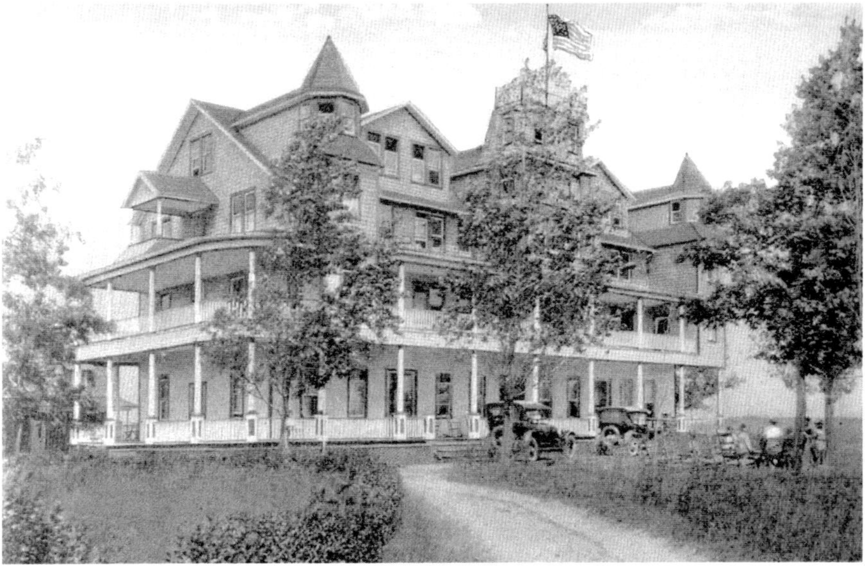

The Lakeside Inn, adjacent to Liberty's Lake Ophelia, as it looked during the Silver Age. Later reconfigured as a Mission-style hotel, the lakeside was eventually purchased by the growing Grossinger operation and was utilized for staff quarters.

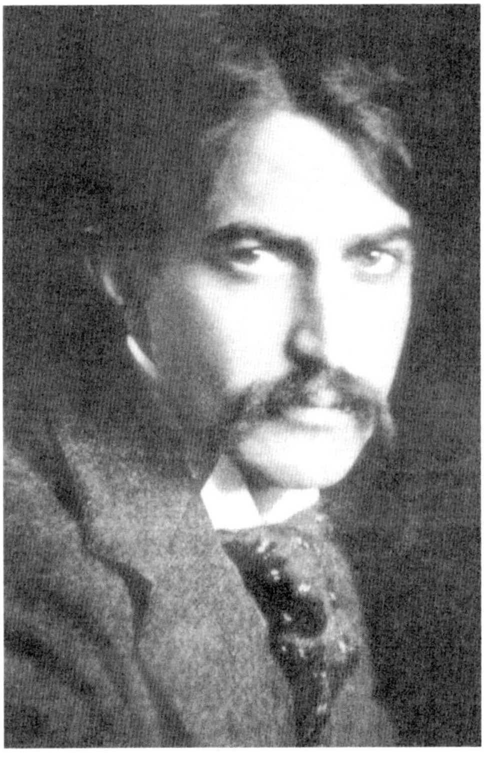

The author Stephen Crane, who grew up in nearby Port Jervis, summered as a young boy at the family's camp in Forestburgh, which the children christened "Saint's Rest." When, at the peak of his fame following the publication of *The Red Badge of Courage*, Crane was asked for biographical information, he wrote, "I live in Hartwood, in Sullivan County, New York, on an estate of 3500 acres belonging to my brother and am distinguished for corduroy trousers and briarwood pipes. My idea of happiness is the saddle of a good-riding horse." Crane lived at the home of his brother Edmund, the caretaker of their oldest brother William Howe Crane's Hartwood Club. Edmund also served as the Hartwood postmaster, as well as the Hartwood stationmaster on the Monticello & Port Jervis Railroad.

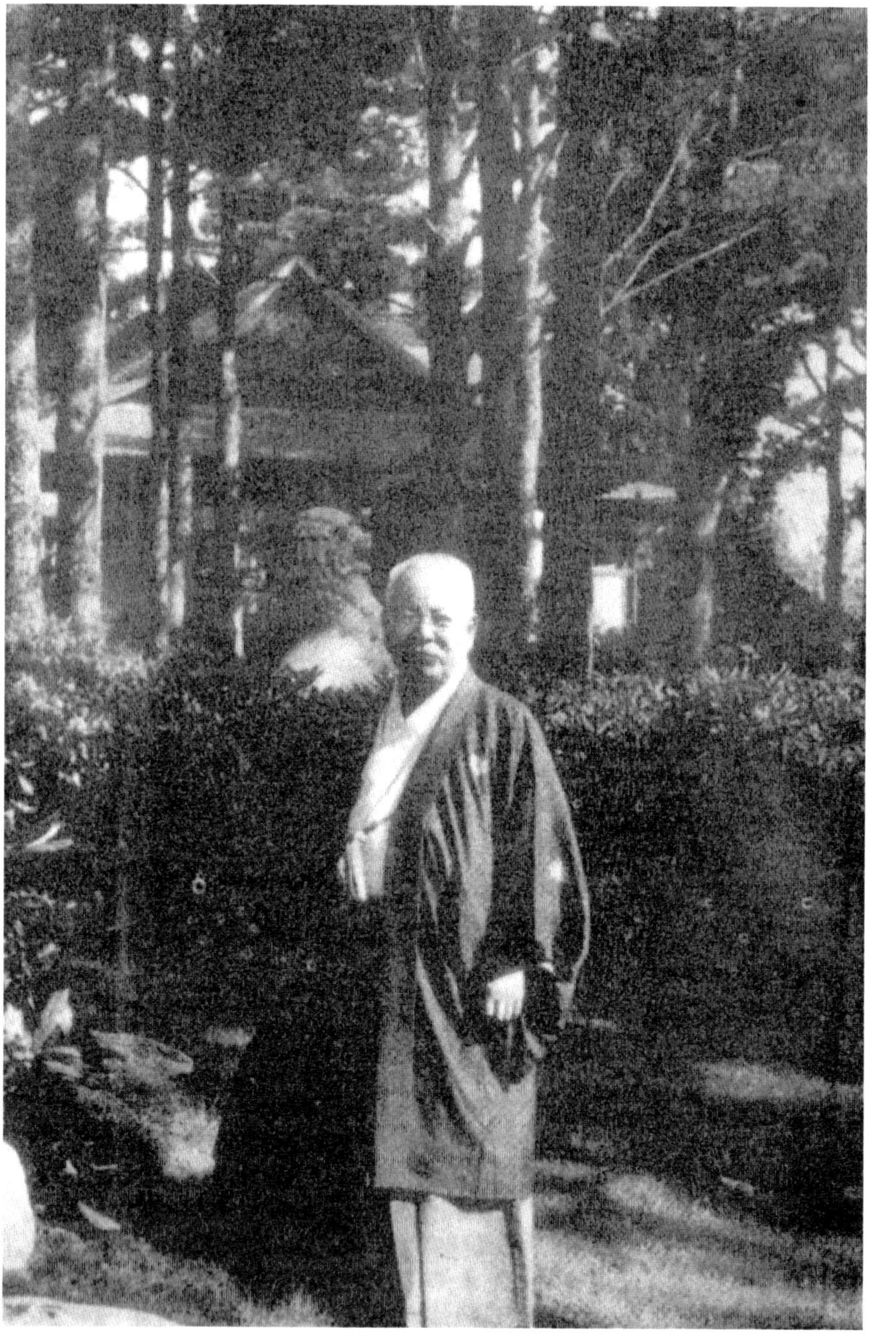

Dr. Jokichi Takamine, who lived at Merriewold Park until his death in 1922. His widow remained until 1932. Takamine also owned a nearby farm, which he gave to the park for use as its golf course. Much of Merriewold had been purchased from the estate of W.W. Gilman following his death.

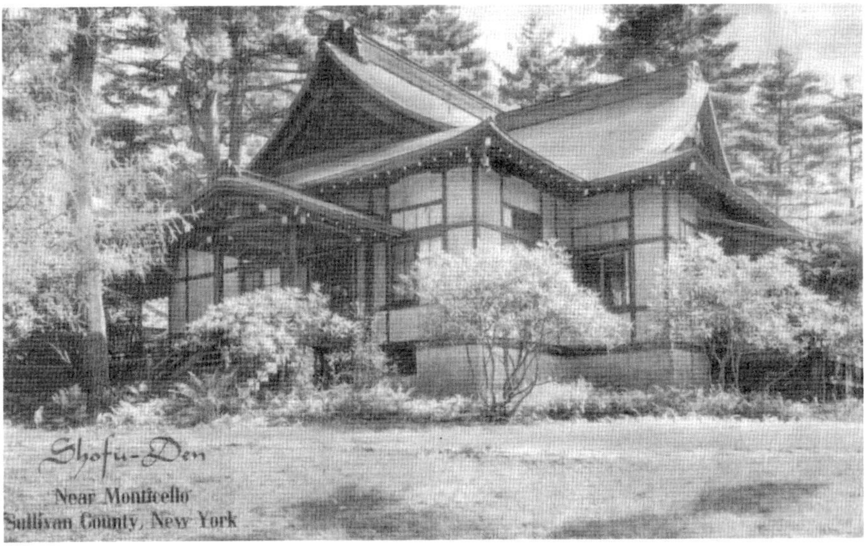

Sho Fu Den, the pine maple palace, was a gift of the Japanese government to Dr. Jokichi Takamine, the Japanese American chemist who synthesized adrenaline, following the 1904 World's Fair in St. Louis. It is the most interesting building among many interesting buildings in Merriewold Park, the colony founded by economist Henry George. Takamine was married to Caroline Hitch, the sister of George's daughter-in-law. The house later belonged to John Moody of Moody's Investor's Service.

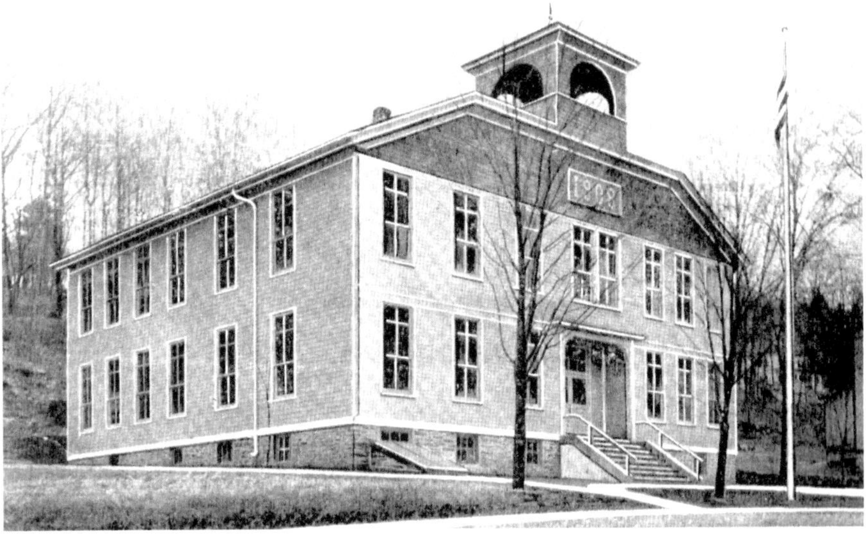

The school at Callicoon. These rural schools were the norm throughout the county, although many were never more than one room. Some continued to be used until the 1950s.

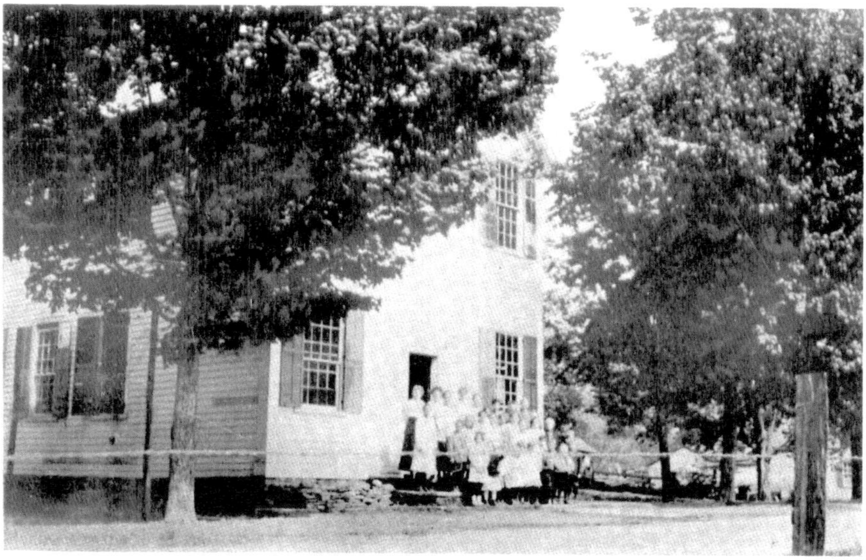

The Callicoon Center school was another fairly typical rural school.

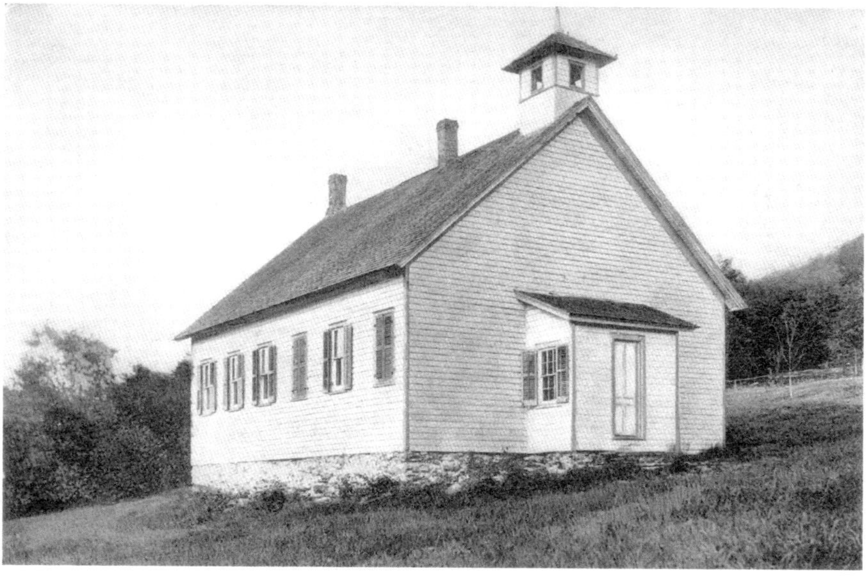

The one-room schoolhouse at Willowemoc.

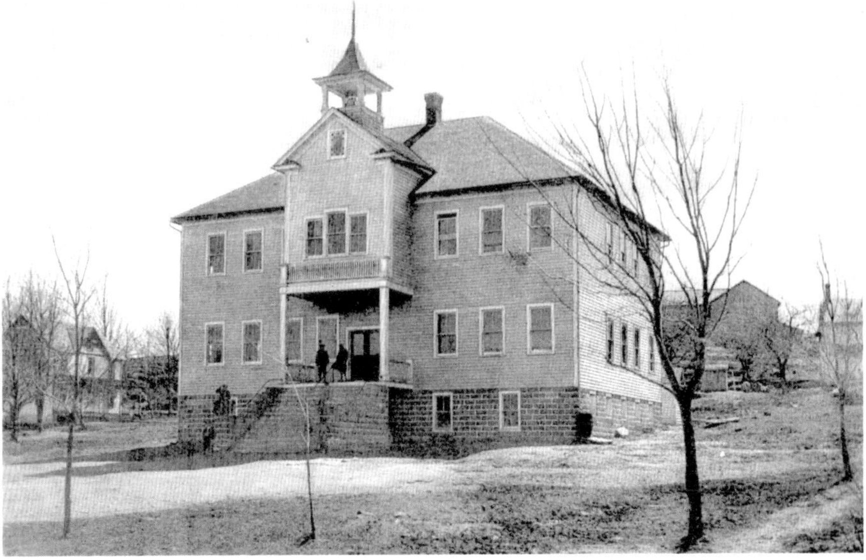

The Centerville School bears some architectural resemblance to the school in Callicoon. Centerville (or Centerville Station, as it was officially known) became Sullivan County's fifth incorporated village in 1911. In 1917, it officially changed its name to Woodridge. Voters approved the expenditure to construct a new school building in 1922, but the building was not completed for another ten years.

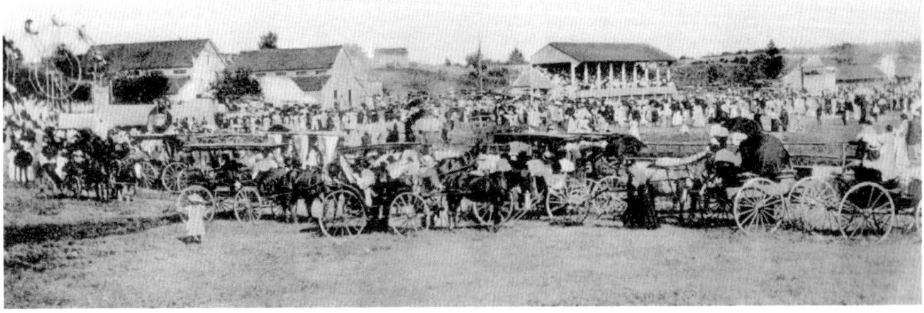

The Sullivan County Fair was held every year in Monticello from 1875 to 1931. Festivities were originally held in the park in front of the courthouse, but the event quickly outgrew that space. It was later held on the fairgrounds on what is today West Broadway. The fair was sponsored by the Sullivan County Agriculture Society, which had been founded in 1855.

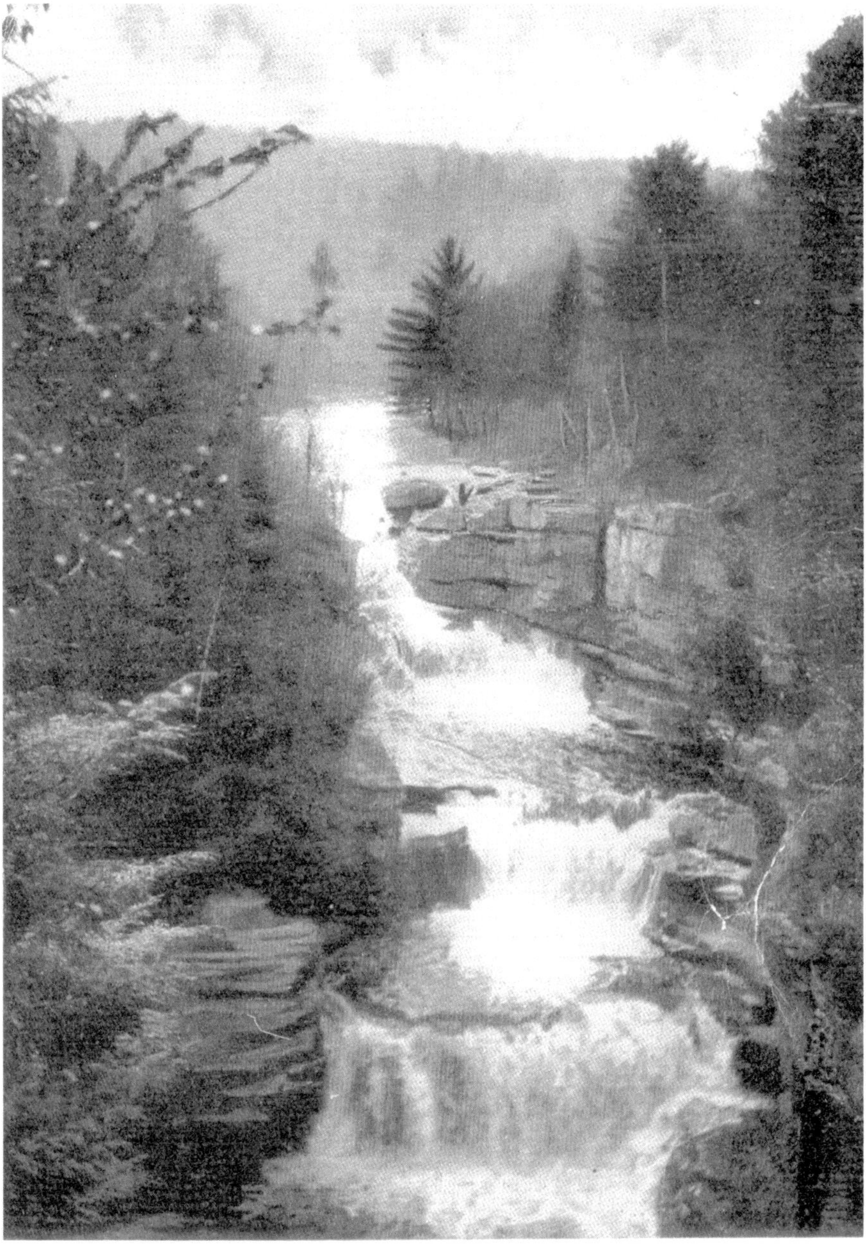

The Mongaup Falls in the town of Forestburgh was Sullivan County's most popular tourist destination in the late nineteenth century, as visitors from all over flocked there to picnic while taking in its power and majesty. Reputed to be the third-highest falls in New York State, it was the worthy subject of two lengthy poems by Alfred B. Street.

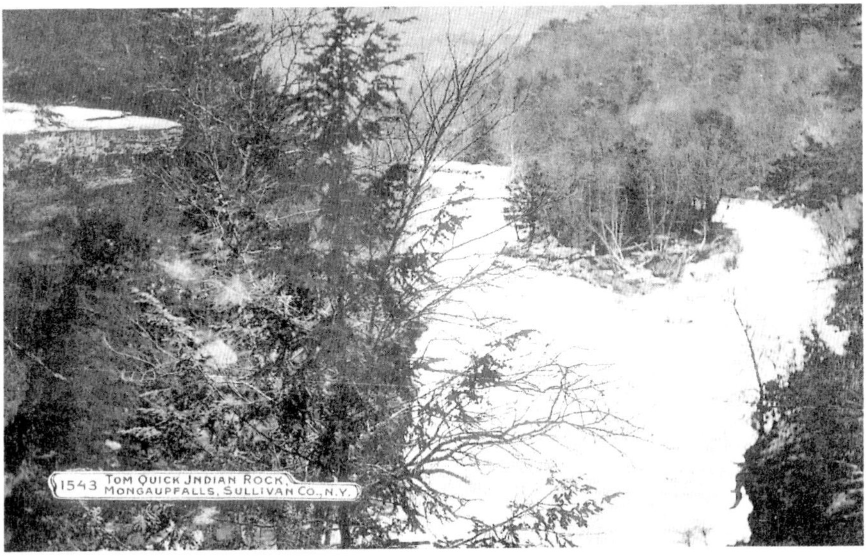

The Mongaup Falls from another vantage point. In his poem "A Visit to the Mongaup Falls," Street wrote, "A deep gorge winds upward and forth with a bound / The cataract's pitch shakes its thunder around / It comes from its shadow'd and prison-like glen / With a leap and a road, like a lion from den." The falls were destroyed by the Rockland Light & Power Company in the construction of its reservoir system.

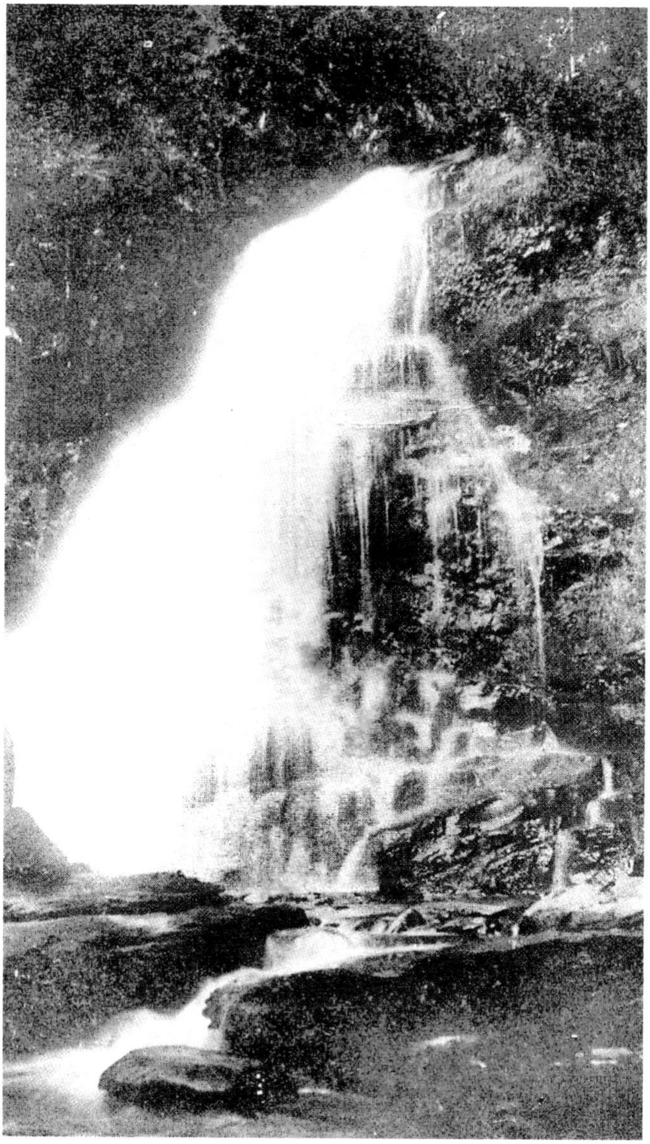

Katrina Falls in Rock Hill was another secluded falls that became a popular hiking destination. Reputedly named for a damsel who took her own life by intentionally plunging over the falls, the area remains virtually unchanged to this day.

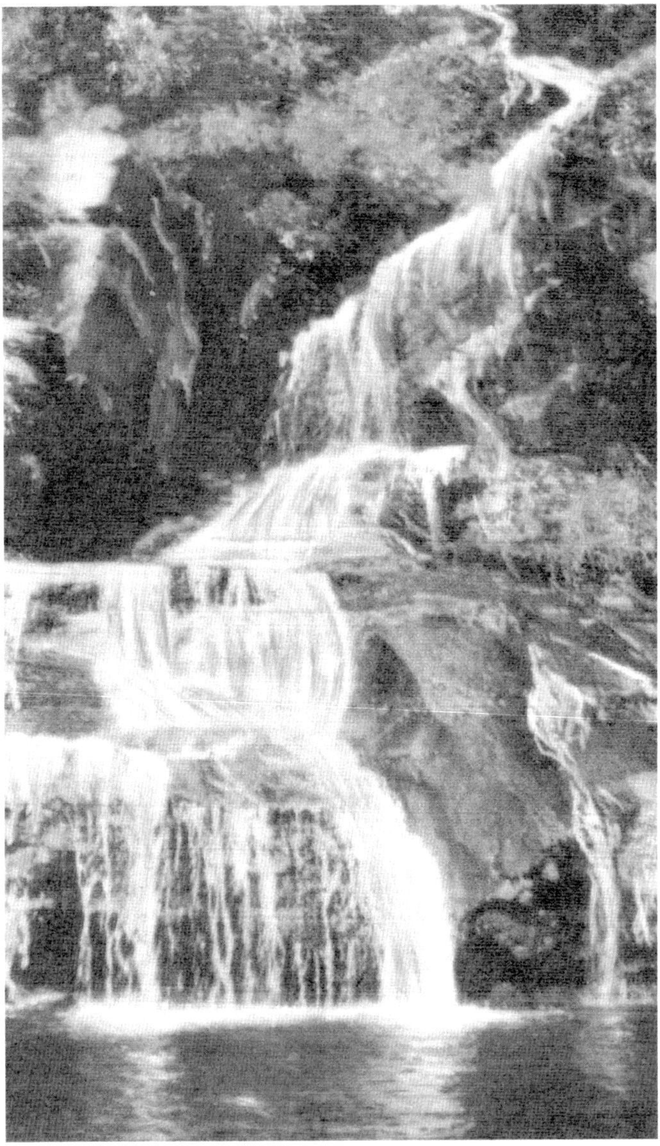

Rashkin's Little Falls Hotel near Mountaindale featured this popular landmark, also known as the "the Niagara of Sullivan County." A promotional blurb described the falls as "noted for its natural grandeur…a picture of scenic beauty and is one of the most beautiful spots in the mountains." It remains much the same today.

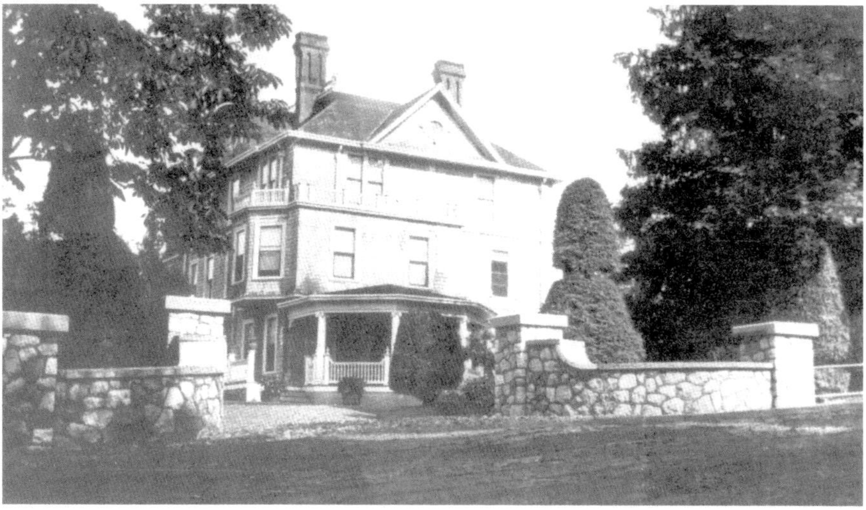

George Ross Mackenzie came to America from his native Scotland and went to work as a mechanic for the Singer Sewing Machine Company. His work ethic and shrewd business mind caught the attention of Isaac Merritt Singer, and Mackenzie eventually became the company's third president, leading it through a period of phenomenal growth. He came to Sullivan County on a horseback-riding expedition in the 1860s and fell in love with the natural beauty of the region. He purchased about thirty-five hundred acres of land near South Lebanon and renamed the area Glen Spey, or "valley of the spring." The Homestead was his castellated mansion, which included terraced lawns, intricate topiary, a pond for swans and a golf course. *Photo courtesy of Frank V. Schwarz, town of Lumberland historian, and the Glen Spey Museum.*

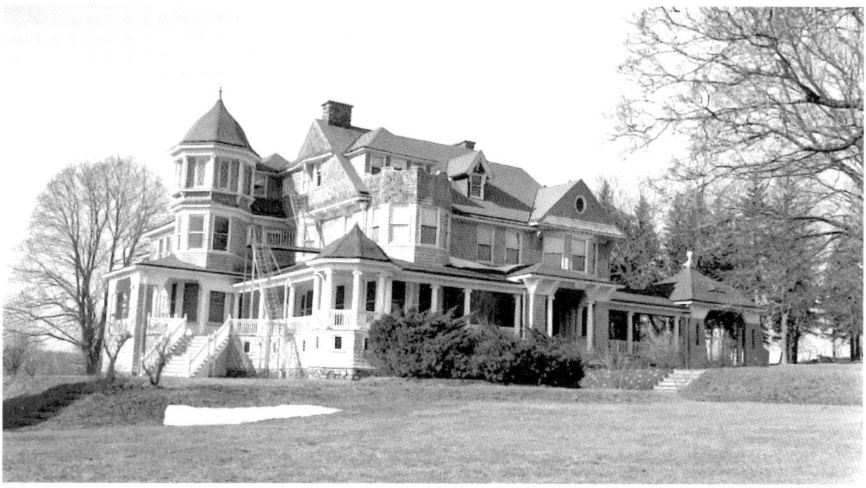

Bramble Brae was one of the mansions built for George Ross Mackenzie's children, in this case, daughter Grace Mackenzie Ewing. This is a later photo of the intricately designed home, which was finally demolished in 1975. Several outbuildings were left standing, though none in good repair. *Photo courtesy of Mountain View Resort Archives.*

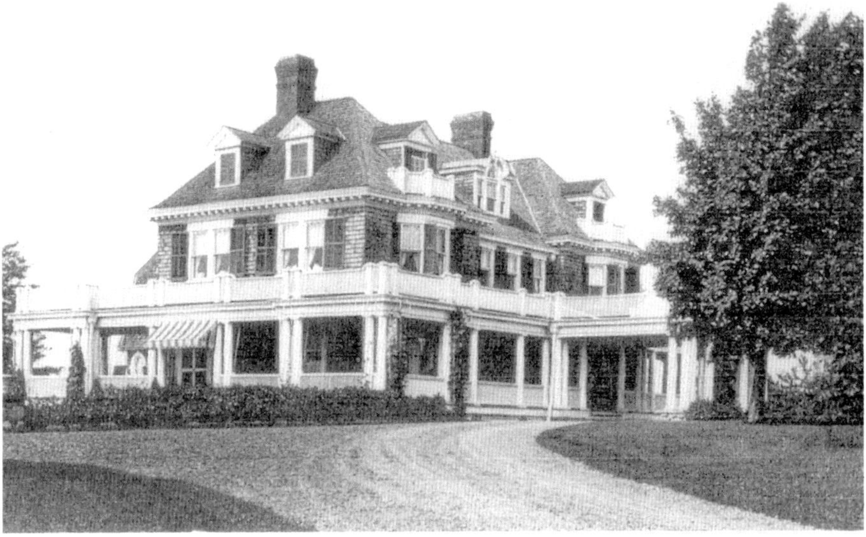

Ardmore, built for Rebecca Mackenzie Vanderbeek in 1891, has survived, though for many years it was virtually unrecognizable due to renovations. It has recently been restored to its original character and serves as the main building of the Mountain View Resort. *Photo courtesy of Mountain View Resort Archives.*

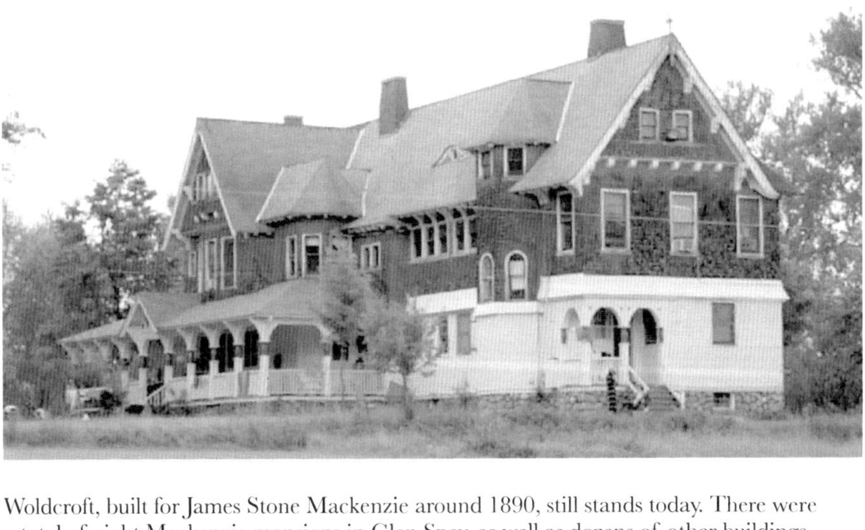

Woldcroft, built for James Stone Mackenzie around 1890, still stands today. There were a total of eight Mackenzie mansions in Glen Spey, as well as dozens of other buildings—gatehouses, carriage houses, servant's quarters, etc.—that have been adapted for reuse.

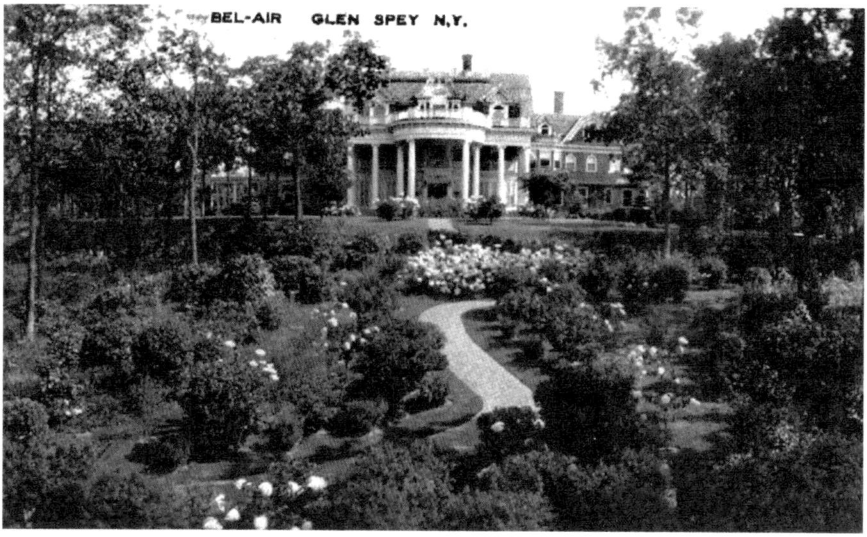

Bel Air, the largest of the mansions constructed for George Ross Mackenzie's children, belonged to Edward Easten Mackenzie and stood imposingly on a hill overlooking the community of Glen Spey. It was destroyed by fire in the mid-twentieth century. *Photo courtesy of Frank V. Schwarz, town of Lumberland historian, and the Glen Spey Museum.*

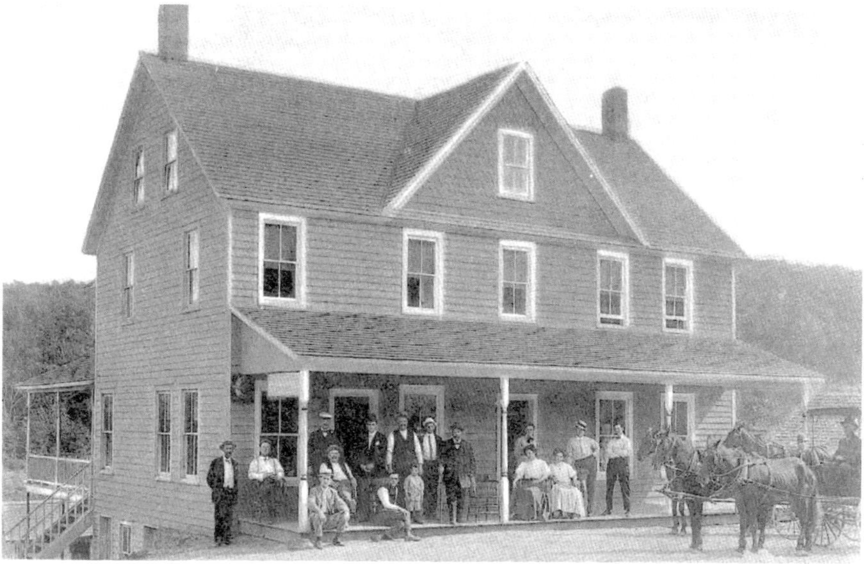

Despite its relative isolation from the rest of the county, and its lack of rail service, the town of Neversink had its share of Silver Age boardinghouses. This is the Riverside, which was fairly typical of the small farmhouse-type accommodations available in the town. *Photo courtesy of Time and the Valleys Museum, Grahamsville.*

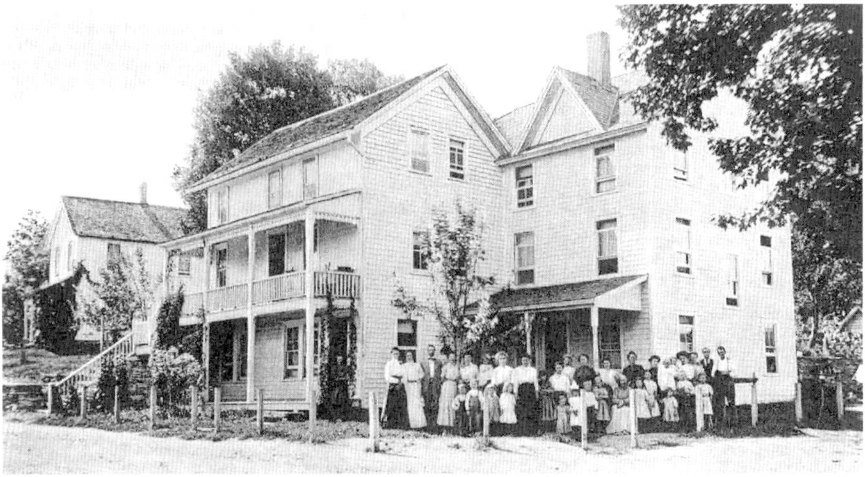

The Edgemere boardinghouse in Grahamsville changed little over the years. While the resorts in the central part of the county underwent drastic revisions during the transition from Silver Age to Golden Age, the boardinghouses and small hotels of the upper Neversink, much like those of the upper Delaware, remained largely unaffected. *Photo courtesy of Time and the Valleys Museum, Grahamsville.*

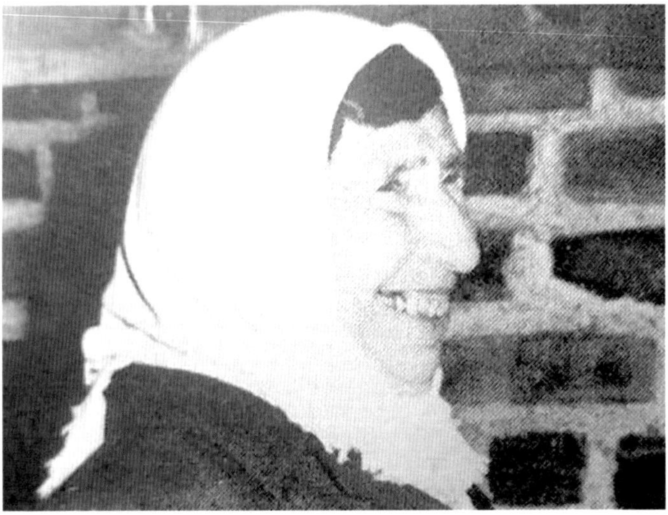

Selig and Malke Grossinger (pictured) brought their family to the mountains in 1914, mainly due to Selig's ill health. They purchased a small farm called the Longbrook near Ferndale with intentions of farming themselves, but they soon found that they could make more money renting out their spare rooms. That first year, Grossinger's Kosher Farm entertained nine guests and grossed eighty-one dollars. With hard work and dedication, and Malke's innkeeping experience and home cooking, they had outgrown the Longbrook site by 1919, despite an addition and the purchase of an adjoining property.

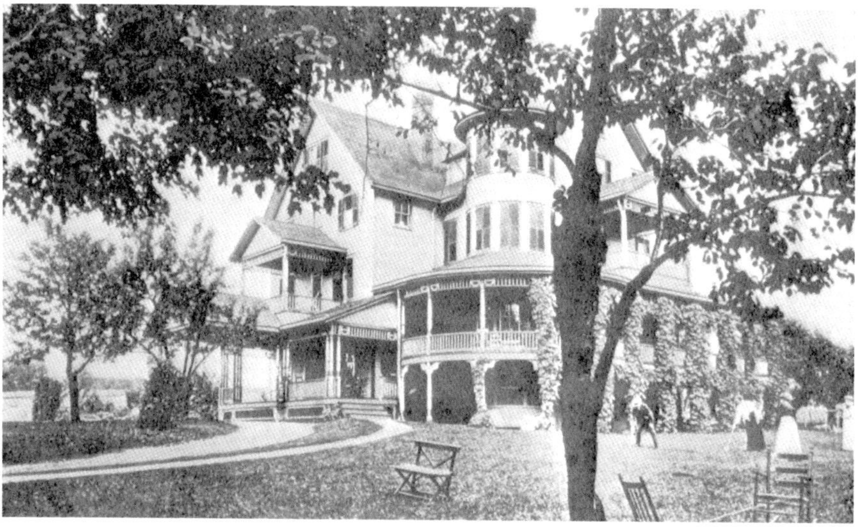

The Grossingers purchased their second hotel from the Nichol's estate in 1919, and the family legend began. Much of the early expansion took place around this substantial building, which was still visible through the 1950s.

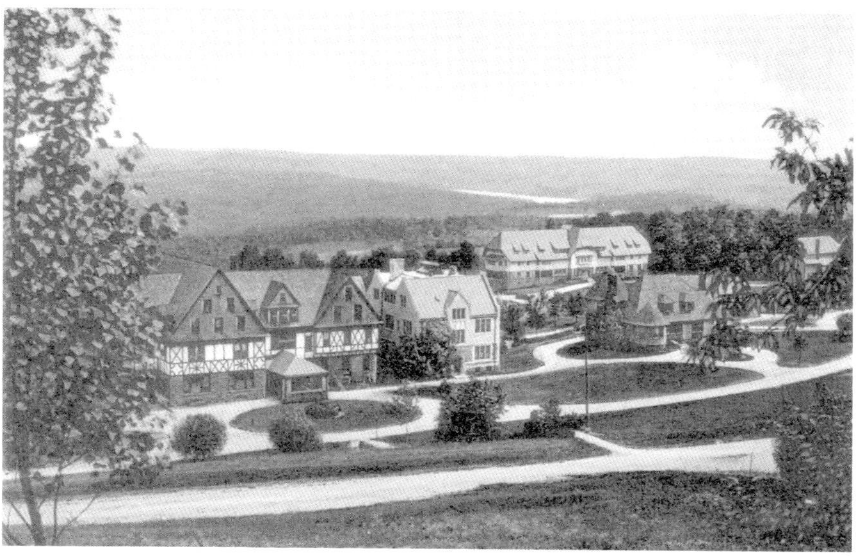

Dr. Alfred Lebbeus Loomis was diagnosed with tuberculosis in 1867. After a healing sojourn to the Adirondacks, he became an advocate of the climatological treatment of the disease and helped found the Adirondack Sanitarium—America's first—at Saranac Lake in 1885. Searching for a location with a similar climate closer to the New York metropolitan area, he settled on Sullivan County, where he purchased land for the erection of another sanitarium. Loomis died in January 1895, before construction could begin, and the facility was completed as a memorial to him. Financed by wealthy donors, including J.P. Morgan, many of the facility's buildings were designed by the most noted architects of the day.

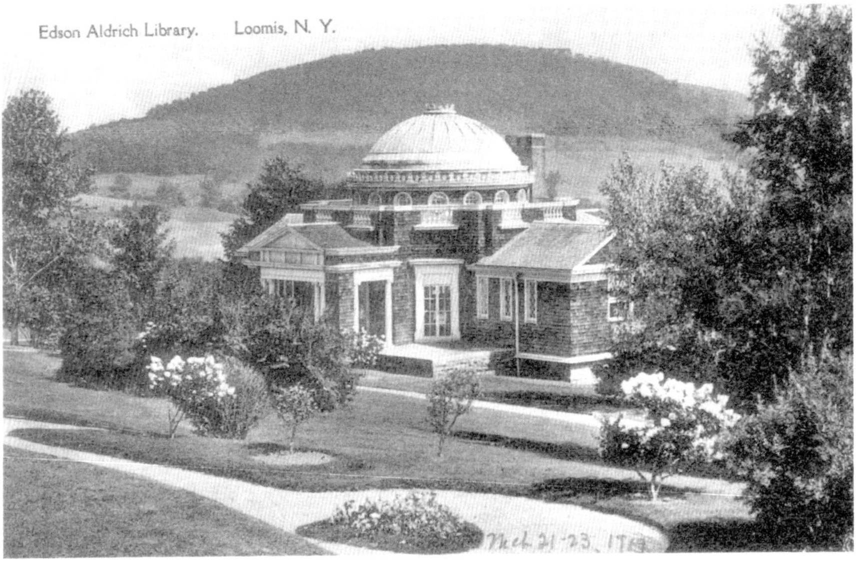

The distinctively styled Edson-Aldrich Library at the Loomis Sanitarium was designed by Fred Wesley Wentworth and built in 1900. The Loomis Sanitarium opened with five buildings in 1896 but grew rapidly, eventually comprising over eight hundred acres and treating 235 patients at a time. The renown of the Loomis operation led to the construction of other tuberculosis treatment facilities in Liberty. The resulting reputation that the county gained as a haven for those with the disease severely impacted the flourishing resort industry and was instrumental in the demise of the Silver Age by 1915.

Chapter 4

THROUGH THE DEPRESSION TO THE GOLDEN AGE

The transition that Sullivan County underwent beginning in 1915 was quite different from earlier periods of transition but no less dramatic. While in the past the county had gone from timber and tanning to tourism, this time tourism would remain the area's principal industry, but it would bear little resemblance to the tourism of the Silver Age.

America itself changed greatly throughout the 1920s. For the first time, the country's urban population exceeded its rural population. That meant more people went on vacations. The automobile became accessible to many, and railroads began to lose their importance. Jewish immigrants crowded into New York City's Lower East Side and eventually found their way to the mountains.

Many of the Jewish families who came here bought farms or took over the defunct hotels of the Silver Age. Slowly, the Victorian hotels of the earlier period took on a new look. Sullivan County Mission architecture started with the construction of the new main building at the Flagler in Fallsburg around 1920 and soon spread throughout much of the county. This style featured a stucco exterior, arched palladium windows and parapets that traditionally sported the name of the hotel in prominent fashion.

These new-style hotels featured structured social activities guided by large staffs, three hearty meals a day and nightly entertainment. Most grew to include multiple buildings, and many began to operate year-round. Golf and tennis, long the staple activities, were joined by skating, tobogganing and skiing, and spectator sports such as basketball and boxing were also offered.

Prominent entertainers who honed their skills while working on the staffs of area hotels included Moss Hart, Dore Schary, Don Hartman, Danny Kaye, Jerry Lewis, Sid Caesar, Jan Murray, Red Buttons, Joey Adams, Van Johnson, Robert Alda, Robert Merrill and Jan Peerce.

Sports legends who worked at the hotels included Buster Crabbe, Pancho Segura, Babe Didrickson Zaharias, Red Auerbach and Wilt Chamberlain. Many other basketball players suited up in hotel uniforms at one time or another, and hundreds of well-known boxers, including Barney Ross, Jimmy McClarnin and Jimmy Braddock, trained at the resorts.

The 538 hotels that dotted the county by 1953 contributed to the growth of adjacent communities. Monticello and Liberty thrived, as did dozens of smaller hamlets from Mountaindale to Roscoe. Businessman Arthur N. Smallwood began selling small summer homes in a self-sufficient development he called Mountain Lakes in 1928. The community eventually became year-round and before long was known as Smallwood.

Sullivan County emerged from the Great Depression and World War II as one of the nation's foremost vacation destinations, forever after synonymous with "the Catskills." This Golden Age lasted from around 1940 to 1965, and the area had never had it so good.

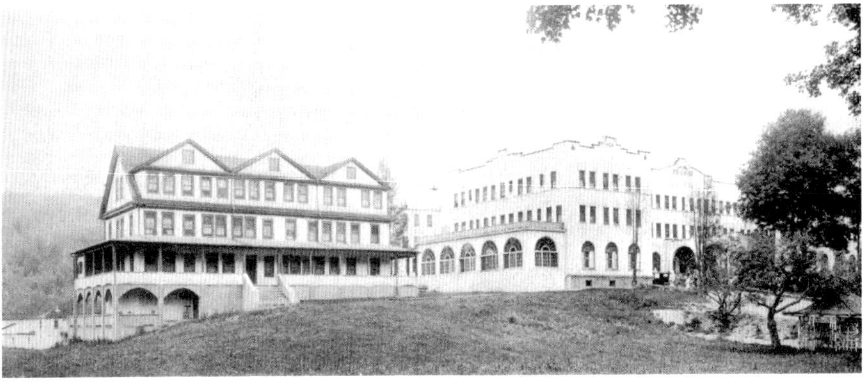

When Asias Fleischer and Philip Morganstern purchased the venerable Flagler House in 1908, they almost immediately began to expand. They learned that many of the guests at the hotel assumed that it was owned or somehow connected to the millionaire industrialist Henry Morrison Flagler, founder of Standard Oil and the man who virtually created tourism in the state of Florida. Not wanting to discourage this notion, the partners decided to construct a new main building in 1919 that looked like one Flagler might have built in Florida. The eighty-room stucco structure (right) was built by Tyrrell and Kinnear of Middletown and cost $175,000. The architectural style was soon being copied by other hotels, and Sullivan County Mission became the style of the era.

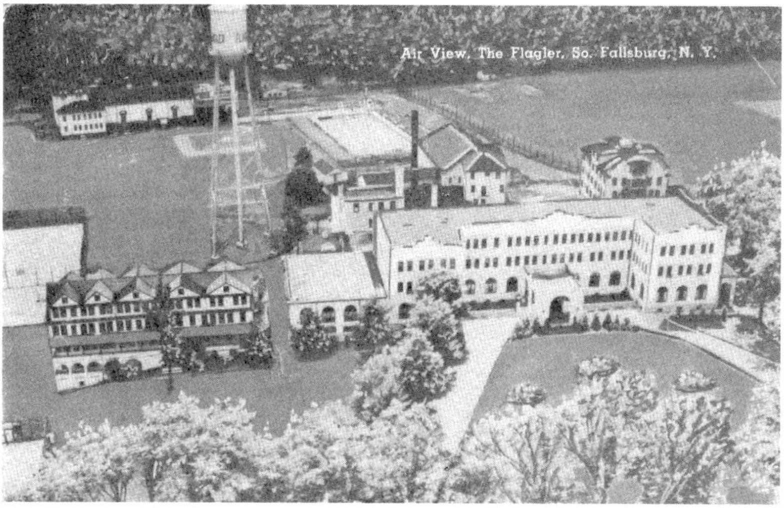

The Flagler was the most prominent Sullivan County resort of the 1920s and '30s and introduced a number of innovations to the county, including hot and cold running water, telephones in every room, fire suppression sprinklers and year-round operation. Franklin D. Roosevelt, unsuccessful candidate for vice president, spoke there in 1921.

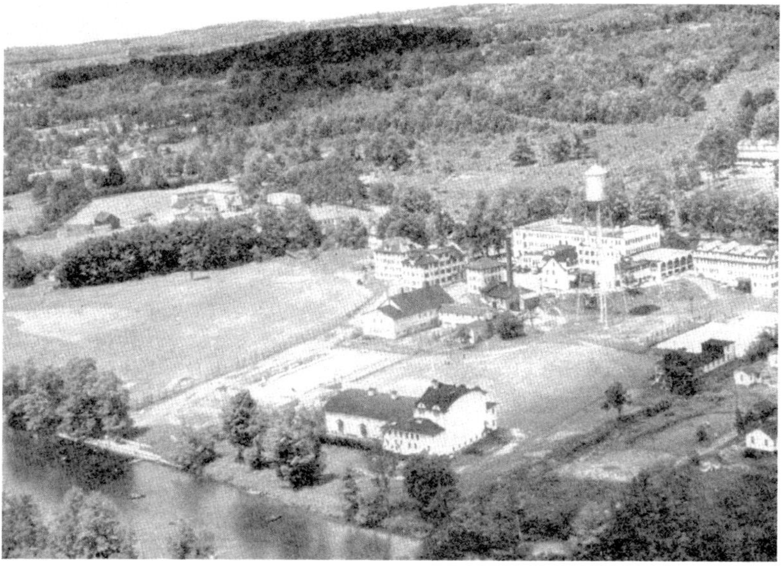

Under Fleischer and Morganstern, the Flagler's location on the Neversink River became almost inconsequential. The hotel featured one of the county's earliest swimming pools, and beginning in 1928, guests were entertained in a state-of-the-art playhouse featuring a talented social staff led by Moss Hart and Dore Schary. The concept of site-independent hotels was proliferated during the Golden Age, when the notion of promoting natural beauty became passé.

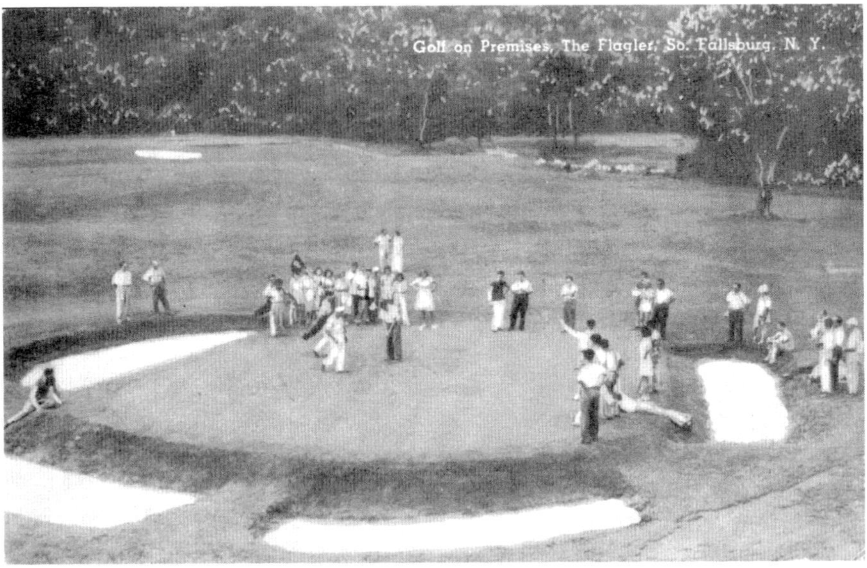

The Flagler's golf course, opened in the 1920s, was not one of the county's first, but it was one of the more elaborate of the early nine-hole courses. The *New York Post* reported that there were three nine-hole courses in the county in 1901; by the early 1960s, there were more than twenty golf courses, many of which were eighteen-hole layouts.

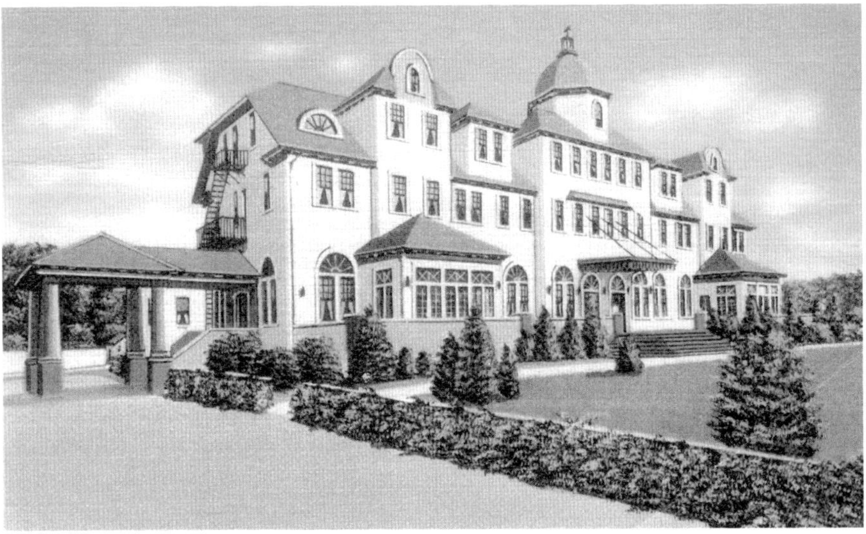

When John Gerson's boardinghouse on Glen Wild Road in Rock Hill burned down, he moved to Fallsburg and built the New Prospect Hotel in 1905. The hotel, which later became the Hotel Levitt (pictured), was located next to the famed Flagler House, and some say that the presence of Jewish vacationers so close to her property encouraged Carrie Flagler Angel to sell her operation to Fleischer and Morganstern a few years later.

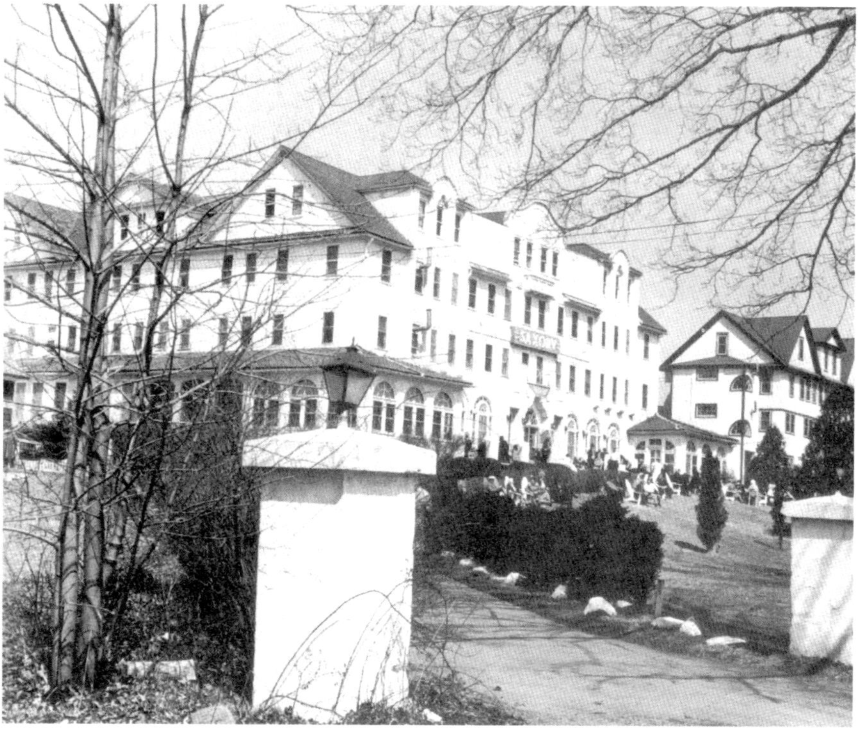

The Saxony, which had previously been known as the Hotel Glass, was across the street from the Flagler and next door to the Ambassador. It was remade in the Sullivan County Mission style, a look that it retained through the 1960s (pictured). It was afterward renamed the Polonia, but the Golden Age having ended, and the promise of casino gaming proving an elusive one, that incarnation was short-lived.

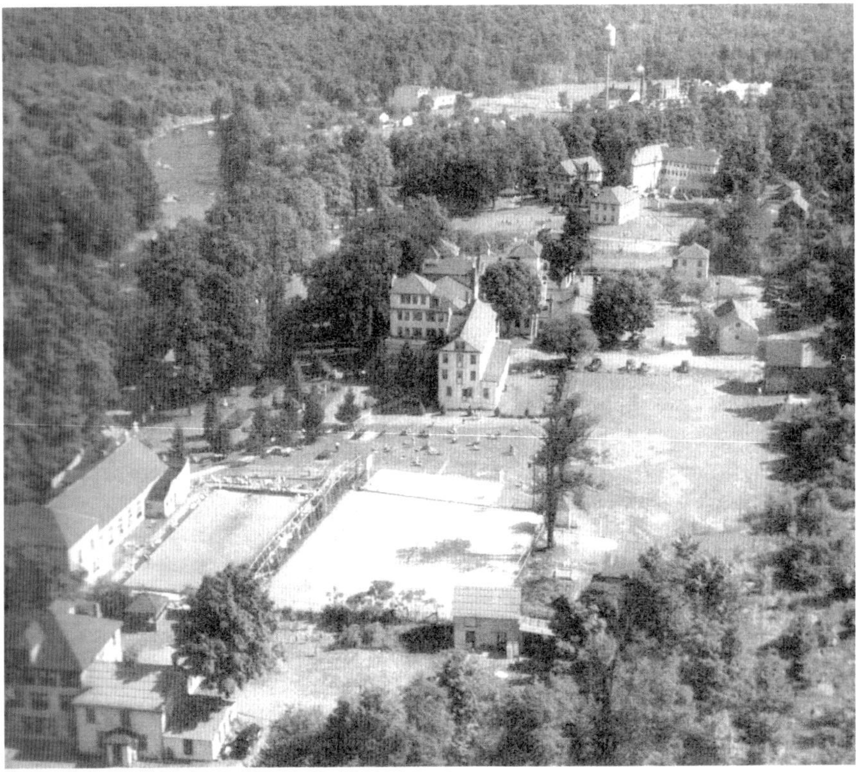

An aerial view of what became known as Hotel Row, along Route 42 between Fallsburg and South Fallsburg. Looking south, we see the swimming pool of the Ambassador, along with the Moulin Rouge nightclub, the Saxony and the Flagler (with the water tank visible) in the distance. These were just a few of the hotels along the route; others included the Murray Hill and the Hotel Furst to the north and the Levitt, the Fallsburg Country Club, the River View, the Elm Shade, the Irvington and the Alpine to the south.

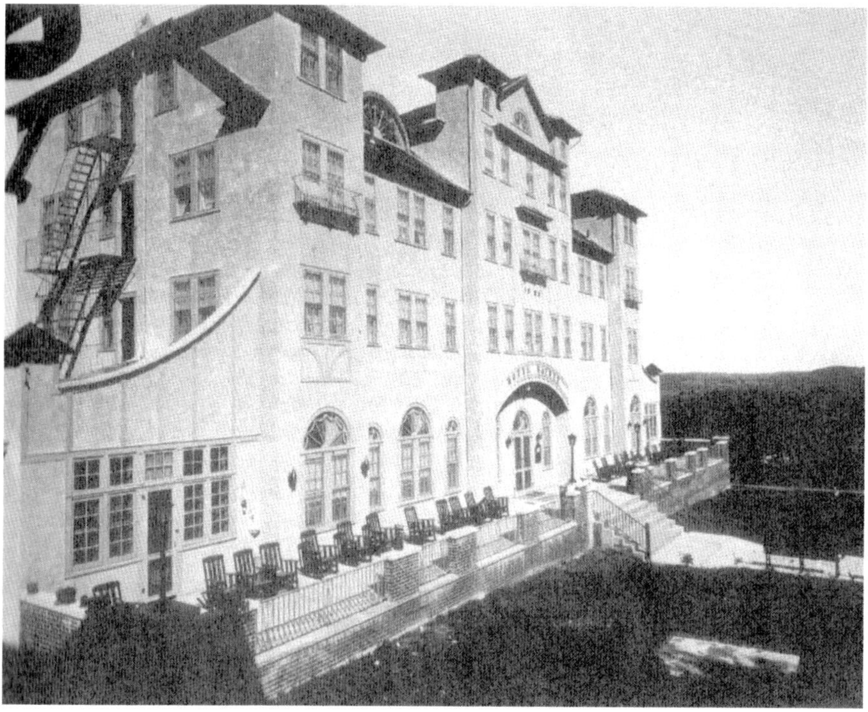

The Ratner later became the Raleigh and as such outlasted most of its contemporaries. Here it is pictured in Sullivan County Mission–style garb, including the stucco exterior, palladium windows and center parapet. The rocking chairs on the porch are a feature left over from an earlier era.

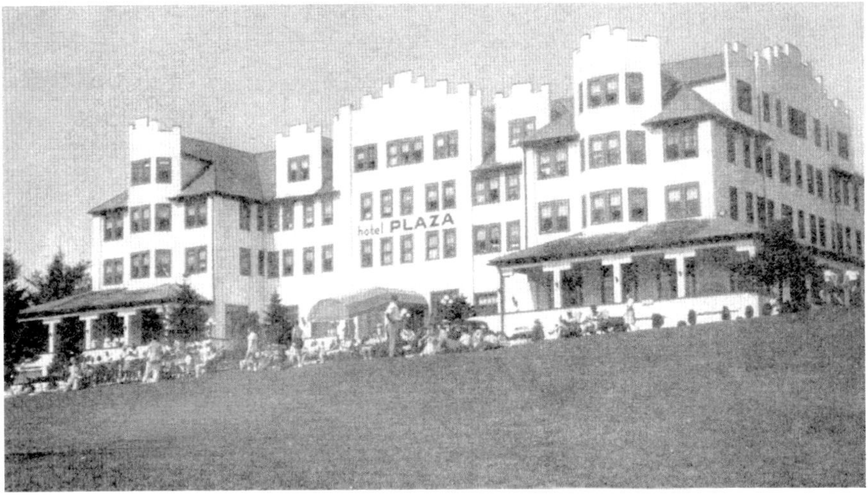

The Plaza Hotel in South Fallsburg was a favorite hangout of the Jewish mobsters who frequented the Catskills in the 1920s and '30s, most notably Louis "Lepke" Buchalter, who put up his mother there for the entire summer some years, and his brawny sidekick, Jacob "Gurrah" Shapiro, who kept his wife and children there while he stayed with his mistress at a nearby resort. The Plaza sometimes featured slot machines in the lobby, an amenity that would conveniently disappear whenever a police raid was imminent.

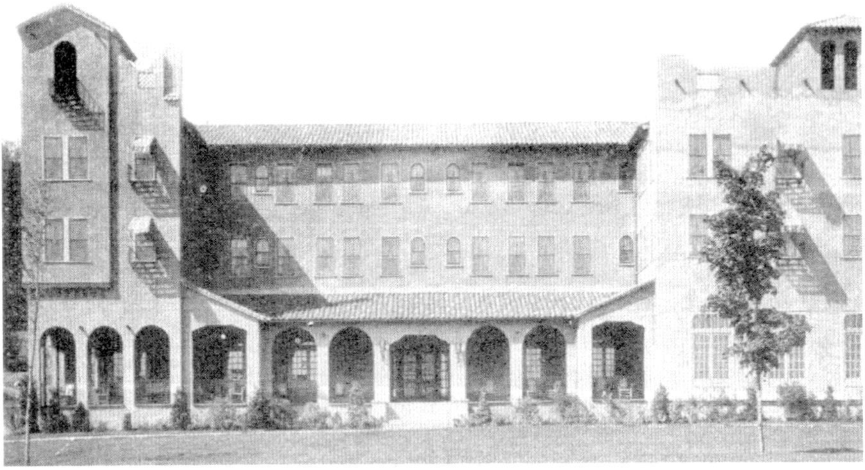

Pauls Hotel in Swan Lake opened around 1910. It once employed an extensive social staff of thirty that included chorus boys, chorus girls, prop men and wardrobe mistresses, all under the direction of Jan Murray. In 1938, a lanky, freckle-faced, blond-haired aspiring actor named Van Johnson played straight man for Murray. By 1940, the hotel accommodated three hundred guests and featured "rooms with bath and shower…new concrete swimming pool…expert instructors in all sports…modern theatre…entertainment and dancing every evening…operas, dramas [and] musicals."

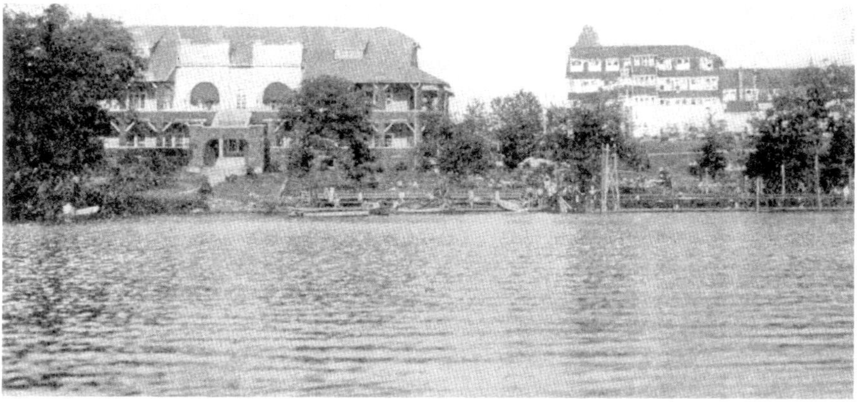

Meyer Weiner founded the White Roe Lake House (or simply the White Roe) in 1919, with just ten rooms. Catering mostly to young folks and stressing athletics and entertainment, it quickly became very successful, opening a state-of-the-art playhouse in 1929. White Roe wasn't the biggest of the many Livingston Manor resorts, but it was probably the best known because of its association with Danny Kaye, who spent six years on the social staff there, honing the unique comedic skills that brought him worldwide fame.

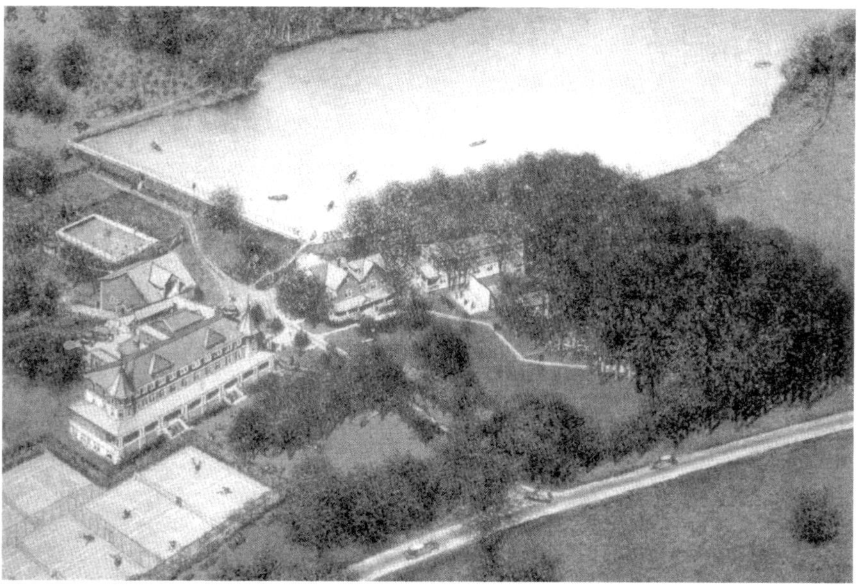

Alex Wittenberg's Edgewood Inn in Livingston Manor featured a private lake and horseback riding with a two-and-a-half-mile-long bridle path around the lake, as well as the usual array of amenities: filtered pool, tennis, handball and badminton courts and an "exceptionally large social and athletic staff," along with "excellent Hungarian cuisine."

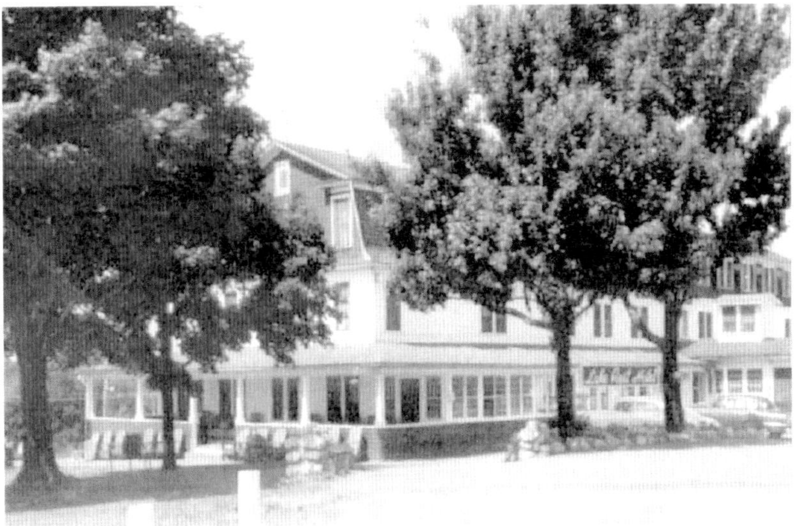

The Lake Rest Hotel, overlooking Sand Lake in Shandalee, was another of the medium-sized Livingston Manor–area resorts. The Lake Rest accommodated 150, and even as late as 1940, when most hotels had moved on to expert instructions in all sports and top-notch nightly entertainment, longtime proprietor T.J. Smith was promising his guests "good food, excellent beds [and] large, bright, airy rooms with running water, milk, cream, eggs, and garden products from our own farm."

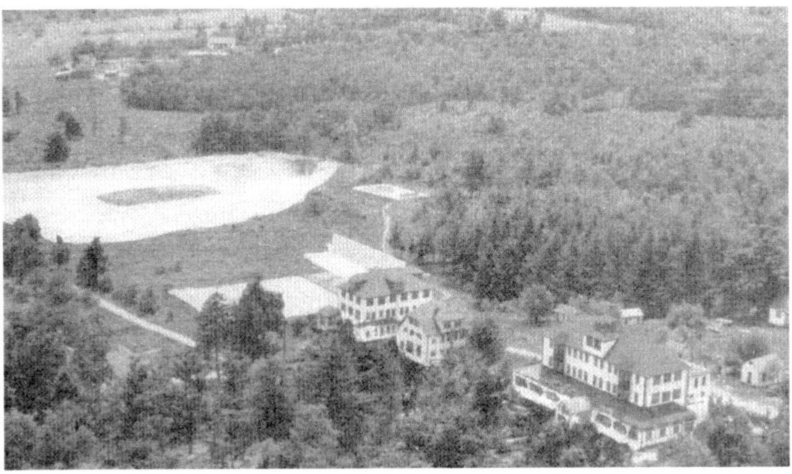

The Gibber family purchased the large Simpson farm in Kiamesha Lake shortly after the turn of the twentieth century and began entertaining boarders. Soon, the hotel had grown to a capacity of three hundred, and while it boasted a "snappy orchestra," a casino and a theatre, calling itself "a honeymooner's paradise," as late as 1940 it was still promoting "fresh eggs, dairy and other food products from our own large 100 acre farm." Gibber's was open year-round for a time and eventually included an indoor swimming pool along with its other features.

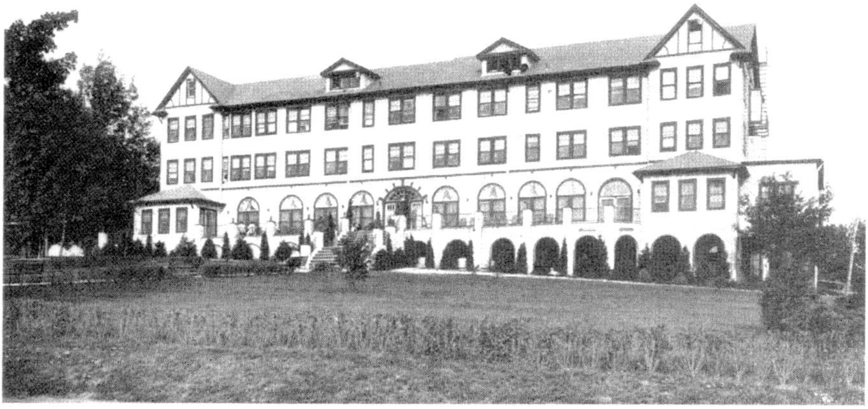

Hair tonic magnate Arthur Winarick bought the Ideal Plaza Hotel in Kiamesha Lake in 1935 and proceeded to build the world's largest resort hotel. From modest beginnings, the Concord Plaza became the New Concord and finally just the Concord. Here, in an early photo, it seems an odd mix of Sullivan County Mission and Tudor architecture, with the palladium windows of the former and the half-timbered gables of the latter.

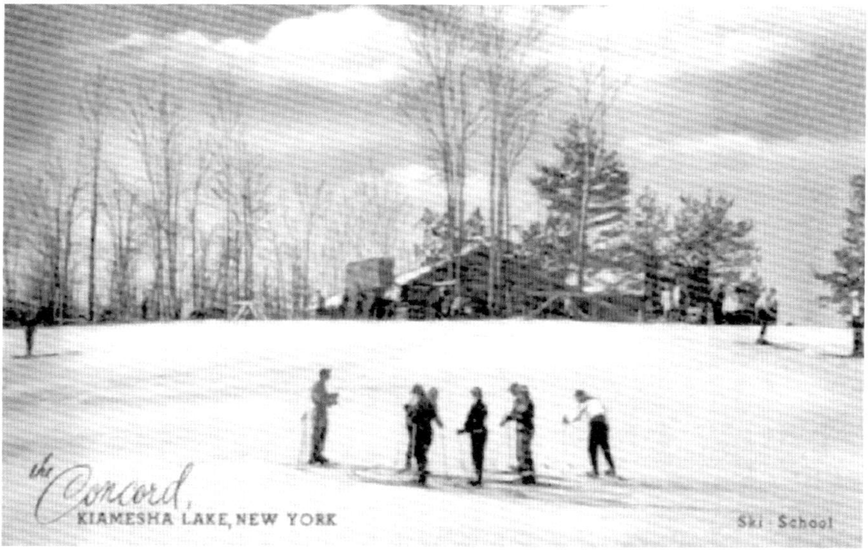

By the 1950s, the Concord was open year-round and promoting skiing in a big way. Only Grossinger's was capable of keeping pace with the Concord's expansion and innovation, and eventually even that fabled resort seemed to be left in the wake.

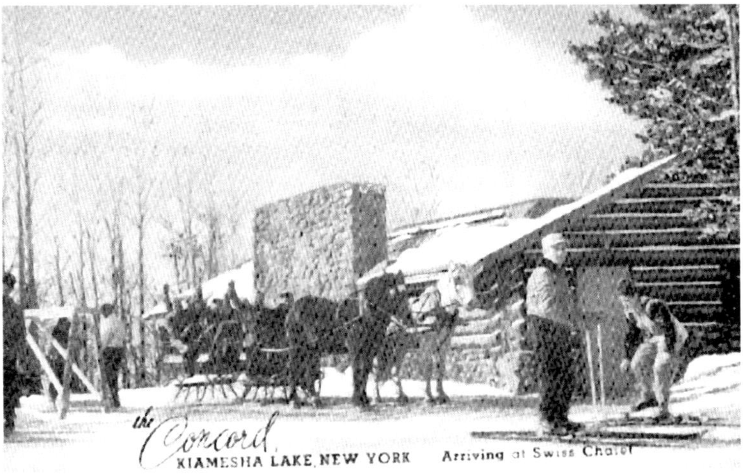

Skiing at the Concord began on a small scale, but by 1958 the hotel had begun making its own snow, often dabbling in different colors. This is the early chalet before a late 1950s addition added twelve hundred square feet encased in thermo glass.

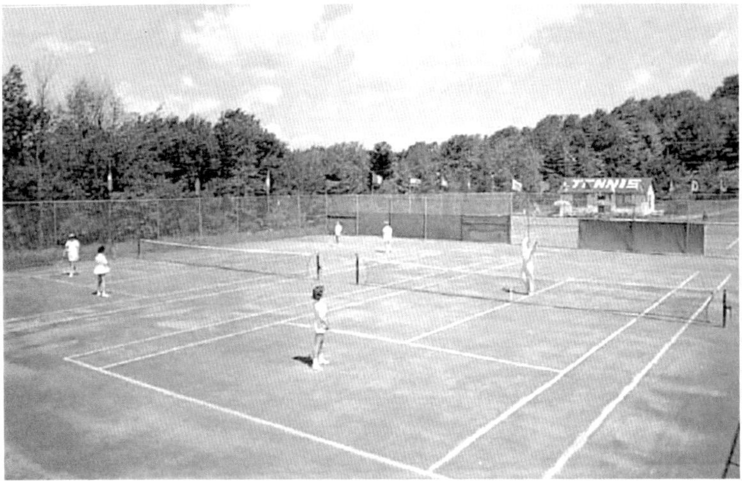

Tennis was big business at the Concord, especially during the tenure of Pancho Segura, a top professional player who augmented his meager salary from the fledgling pro exhibition circuit by teaching at the hotel for ten dollars an hour. The clay courts and crude tennis shack shown here were eventually replaced with one of the largest tennis complexes in the Northeast, comprising sixteen indoor and twenty-four outdoor fast-surface courts. Many of the best players in the world, including Don Budge, Jack Kramer, Pancho Gonzalez, Chuck McKinley, Rod Laver, Ken Rosewall and John McEnroe, played at the Concord over the years.

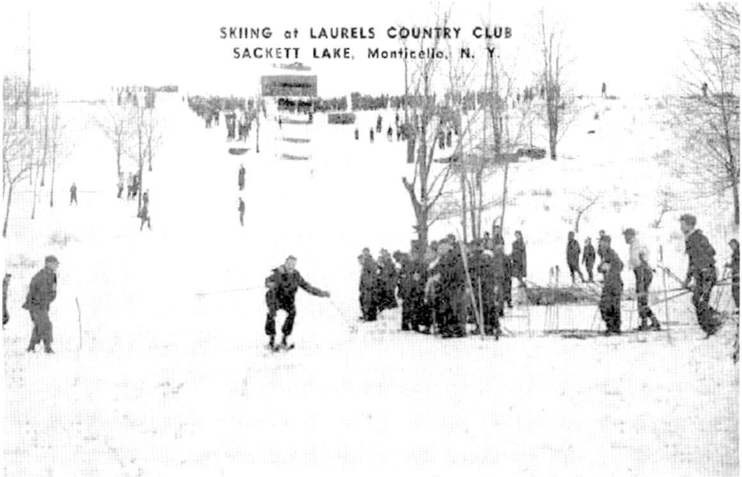

The Laurels on Sackett Lake, a few miles from Monticello, was, for a time, the largest hotel in Sullivan County in terms of accommodations. It was a rival of Grossinger's before the Concord reached that level, and as two of the only hotels in the county heavily promoting winter sports, the Laurels and Grossinger's once went to court over the services of speed skater Irv Jaffe. The Laurels had a rudimentary ski facility when the concept was still fairly new, at least in Sullivan County.

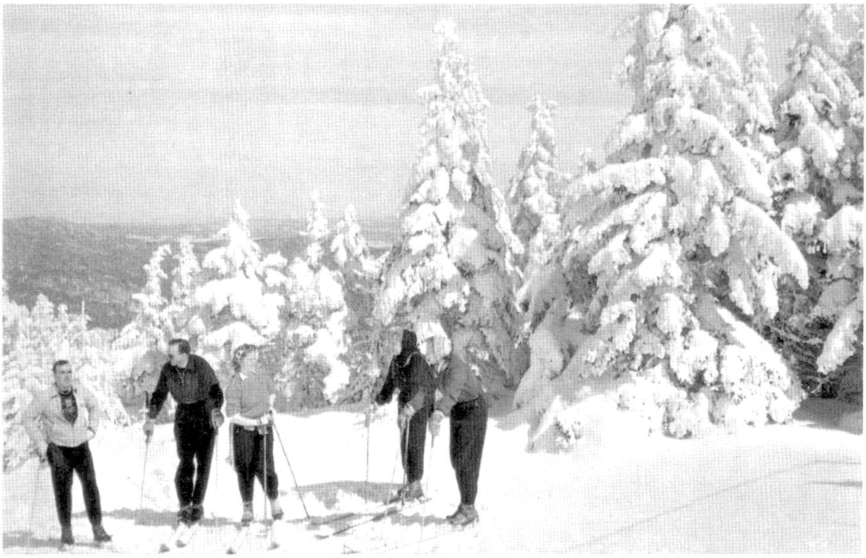

The Laurels' location was as beautiful as that of any Sullivan County resort, and although that distinction became moot as the Golden Age moved into full swing and the notion of the countryside became passé, the ski facility still featured some breathtaking views.

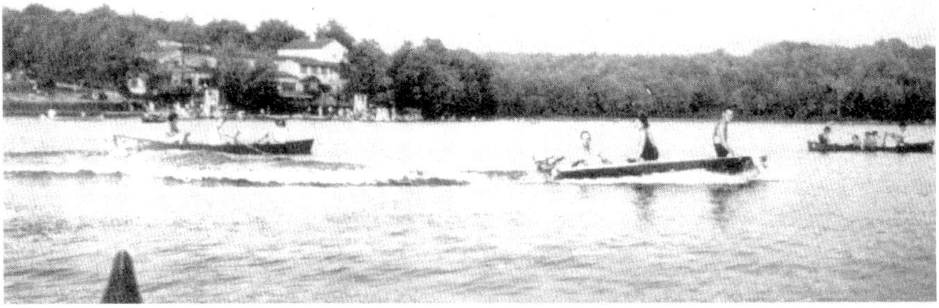

For a time, the Laurels took full advantage of its location on Sackett Lake, and guests often utilized the lake for boating and even waterskiing. In winter, guests could skate or, in keeping with the Golden Age emphasis on spectator sports, watch speed skating races and exhibitions on the lake when temperatures would allow. For a time, Olympic qualifying races were held at the hotel.

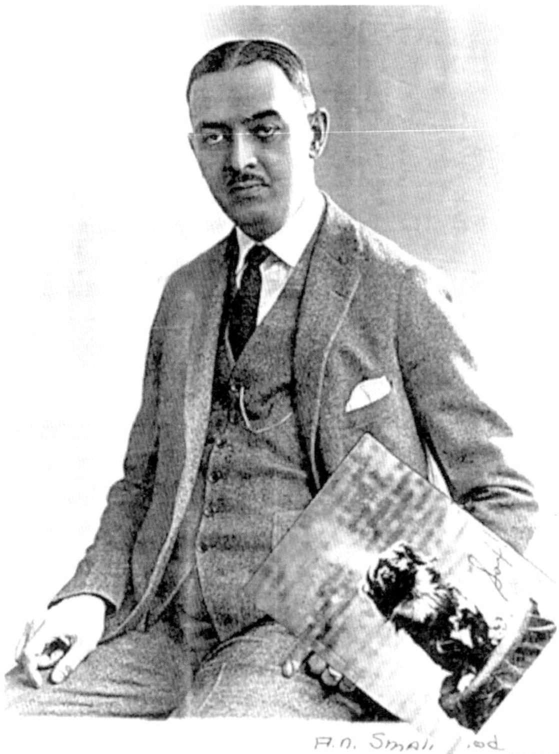

Arthur N. Smallwood (pictured with his dog, Sox) came to Sullivan County from Cincinnati in 1928 and began selling memberships in a summer home community that he called Mountain Lakes Country Club. An early promotional pamphlet promised prospective homeowners, "Here, in a mountain paradise, free from the distractions of the outside world, you will know you have found what you have been seeking. Here you will find smiling faces and contentment at every turn. Here you will quickly realize why so many lasting friendships are developed at Smallwood, and why very few people who visit it fail to make it their vacation home for all time." The pamphlet also noted, "We have a community which is and will always be Christian."

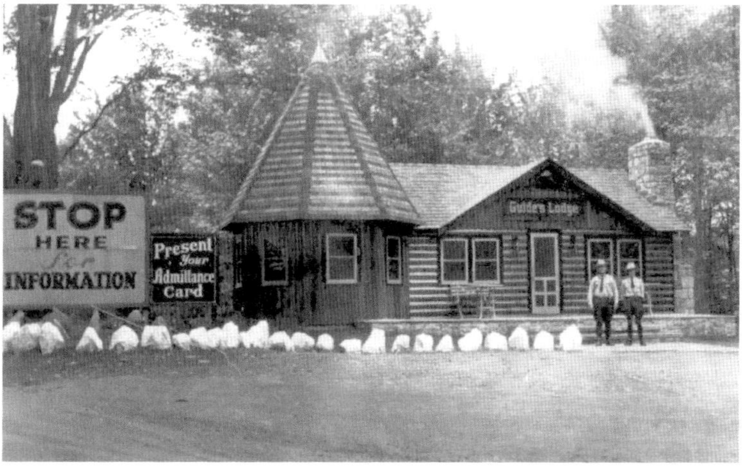

Like at any private club, access to Smallwood was to be gained only after checking in at the front gate. Additionally, the property was patrolled by a horseback-mounted and uniformed security force. Part of the security was no doubt due to A.N. Smallwood's published desire to have "the right sort of people as neighbors."

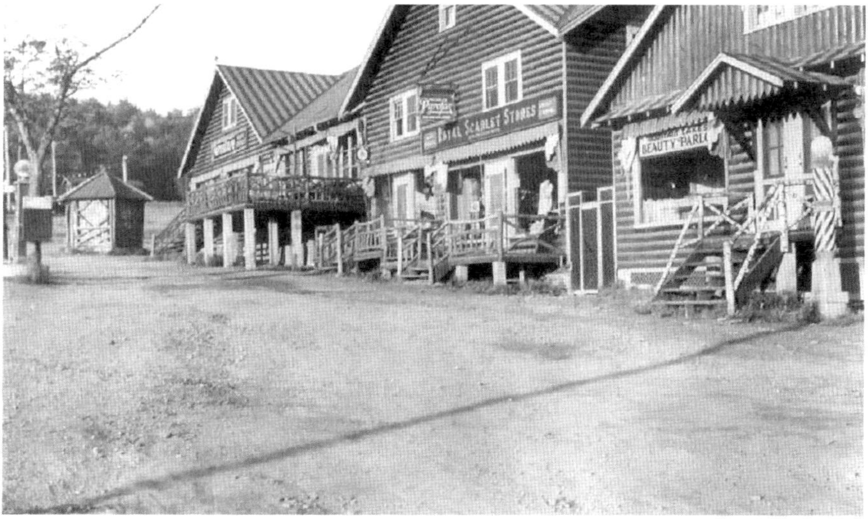

The community that quickly became known simply as Smallwood comprised a post office, community lodges, cabins where relatives of members could stay for a fee, a departmentalized community store carrying everything from home furnishings to groceries, a barbershop, a beauty parlor, an outdoor movie theatre, a golf course, a swimming pool, a tennis court and a lake for fishing and boating.

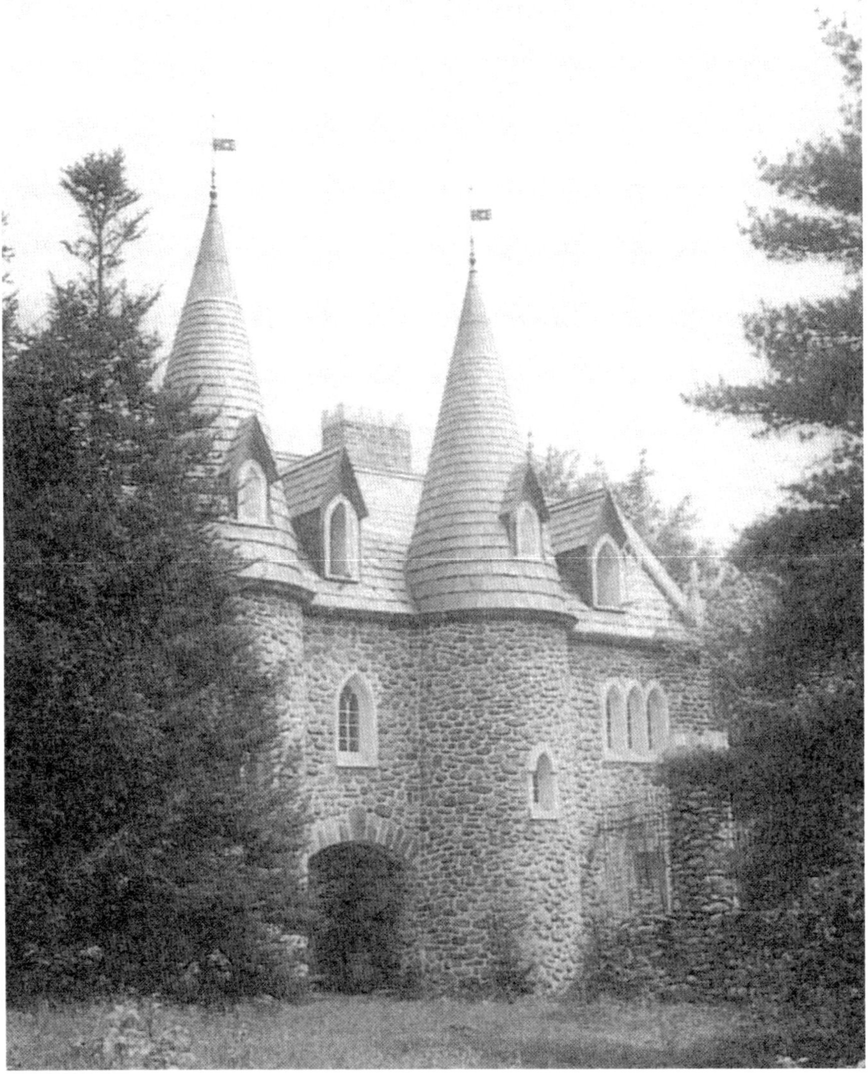

Ralph Wurts-Dundas, the grandson of William Wurts, who had organized the D&H Canal, came to Craig-e-Clare around 1915, purchasing the tract of land that had once belonged to the architect Bradford Lee Gilbert, high on a hilltop overlooking the Beaverkill. It was, in fact, Gilbert's wife, a native of Ireland, who named the community (Craig-e-Clare means "beautiful mountainside"). Wurts-Dundas began construction of an elaborate castle, replicating one he had seen in Scotland, but died in 1921 before the castle was completed. Wurts-Dundas's wife had been confined to an institution, and no one has ever lived in the castle, which remains eerily perched on its bluff to this day.

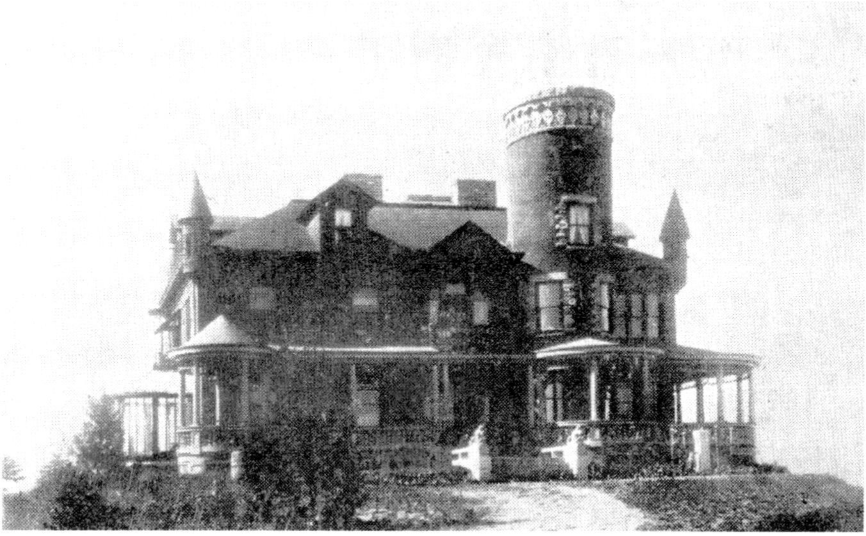

Above: Rudolph Muller was a real estate magnate from New York City who built an elaborate, castle-like home on Egg Hill outside Monticello in the early 1900s. His wife, Elizabeth Worth Muller, was a suffragist of some note and once met with Calvin Coolidge at the White House. One of the Mullers' two daughters married the stage actor Frank Wupperman, who later moved to Hollywood and took the name Frank Morgan. His lengthy list of film credits included portraying the wizard in *The Wizard of Oz*.

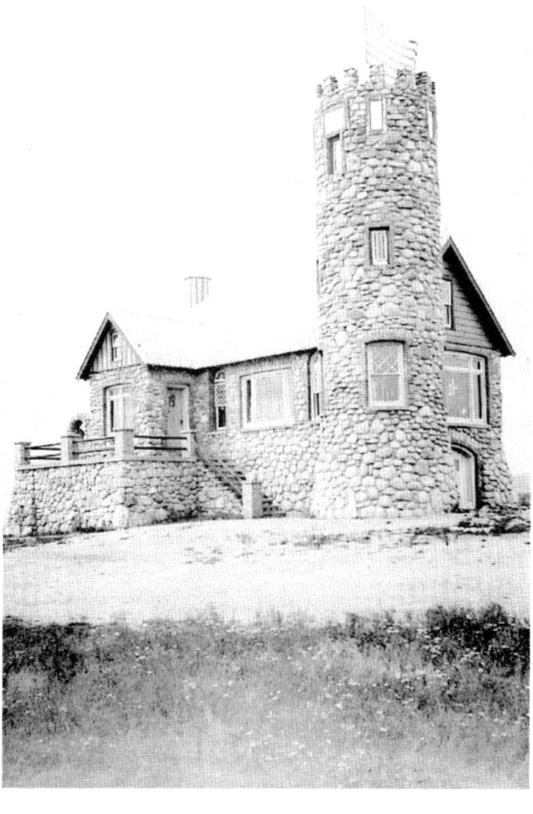

Right: Liberty resident Otto Hillig, a photographer of some renown, aviator, automobile enthusiast and politician, built this castle entirely of local river stones on Washington Mountain overlooking the village. The top of the mountain was once clear-cut, but Hillig planted a number of trees around his unusual home, and today it is completely obscured from view.

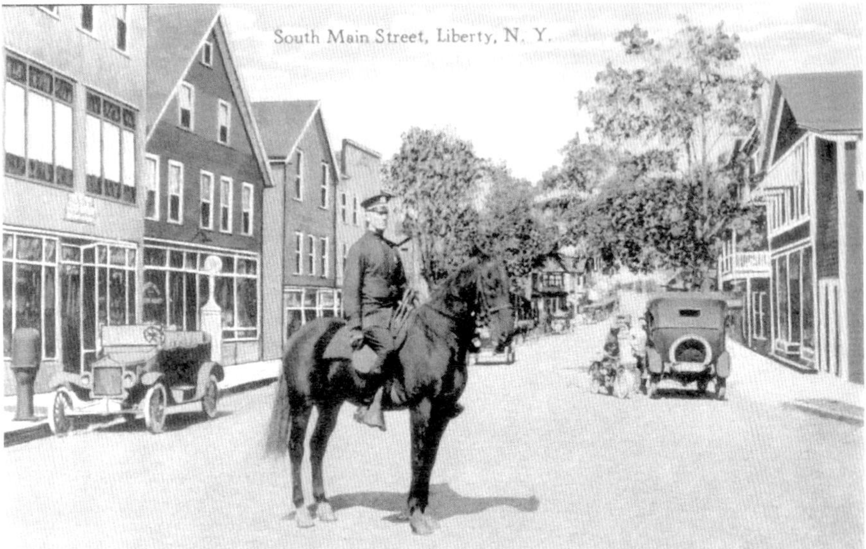

Liberty, one of the county's oldest communities, became an incorporated village in 1870, making it the fourth such entity in the county. Once home to dozens of Silver Age hotels, as well as several tuberculosis treatment facilities, it suffered a major fire on Friday the Thirteenth in June 1913. The fire destroyed half the village's business district, causing an estimated $500,000 in damage. This portion of South Main Street was not affected by the blaze.

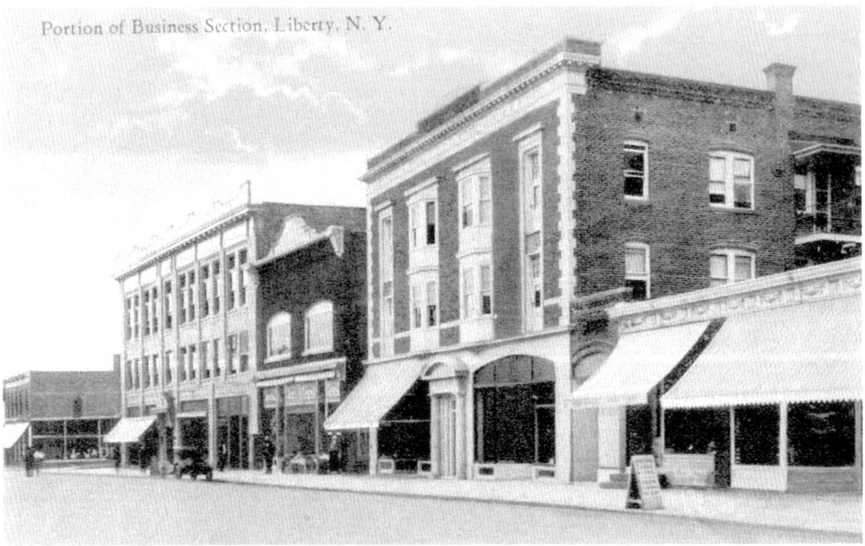

In the wake of the disastrous fire, brick became the construction material of choice along Liberty's Main Street, as can be seen here. Contrast this with the wood-frame buildings in the previous photo of South Main Street.

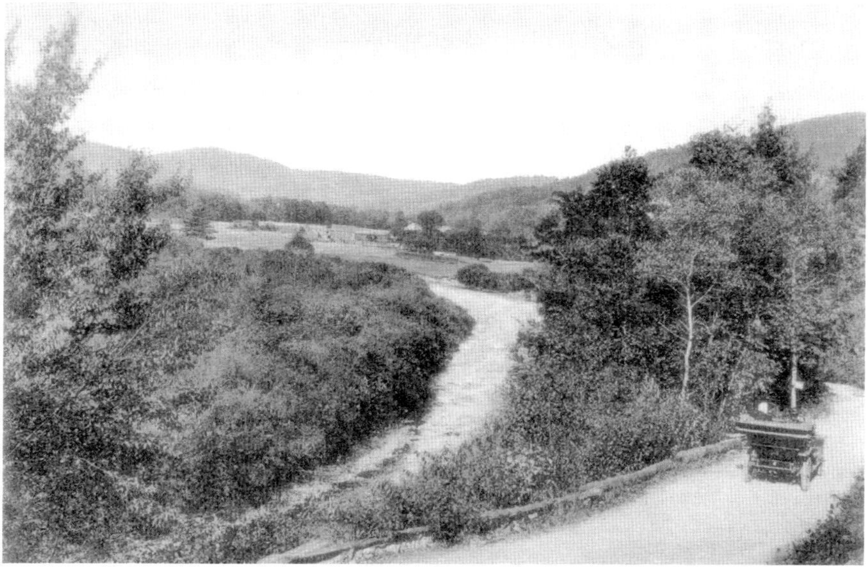

While the central part of the county was caught up in the fast-paced lifestyle of the Golden Age and its hundreds of hotels, some parts of the region were unaffected. Claryville, for example, which grew up around a large tannery in the mid-nineteenth century, had changed little—except for the closing of the tannery—by the middle of the next century.

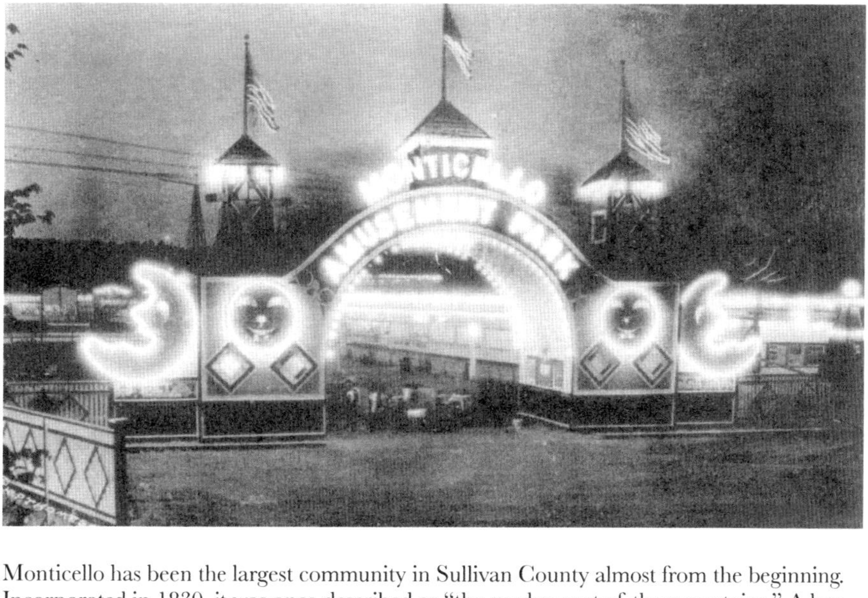

Monticello has been the largest community in Sullivan County almost from the beginning. Incorporated in 1830, it was once described as "the garden spot of the mountains." A key tourist attraction in the 1920s was the Monticello Amusement Park, which featured one of the longest roller coasters in the state and a magnificent dance hall. The park suffered a devastating fire in 1932 and never reopened.

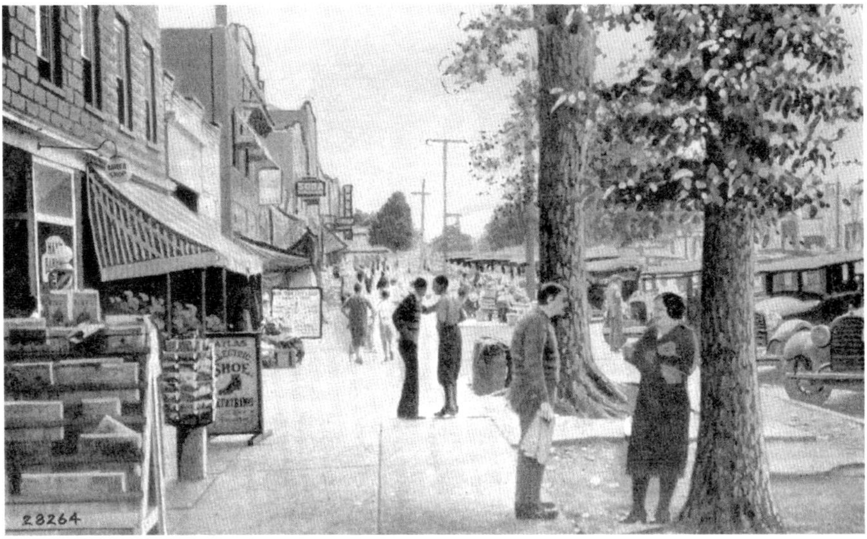

Monticello's Main Street became Broadway about 1920, and the name wasn't the only change taking place. By that time, many of the village's old-time merchants had sold or closed their businesses, and new shops and stores, many owned and operated by newly arrived Jewish residents, had taken their place. This postcard view of a section of Broadway is entitled "the ghetto" for unexplained reasons.

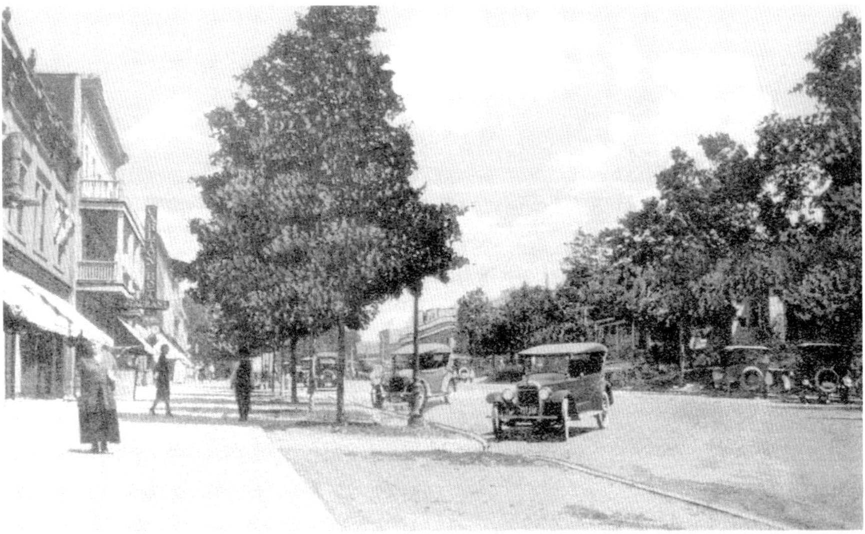

Monticello's Main Street, or Broadway, has been redefined by two major fires, in 1909 and 1919. This photo from the 1920s shows the Carlton Hotel and the area bridging the sections impacted by those two fires.

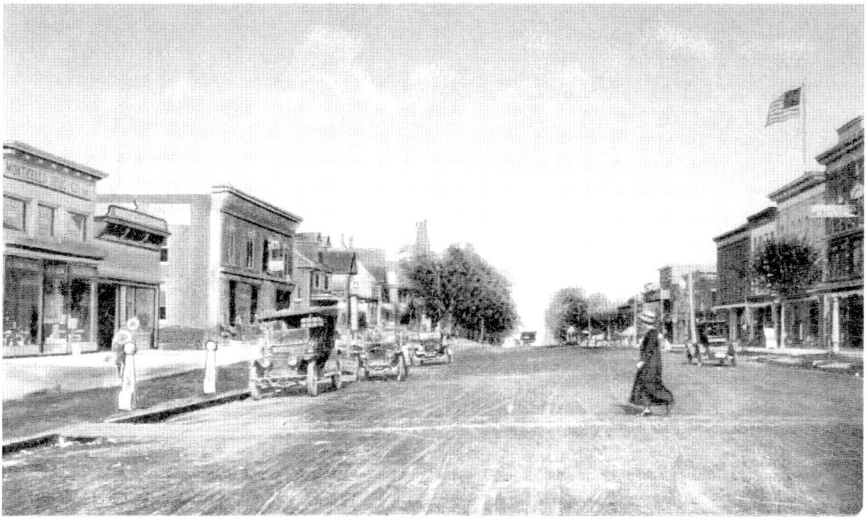

A photo of Broadway, Monticello, showing curbside gas pumps in the foreground and the Methodist church in the background and emphasizing the section of town rebuilt after the 1909 fire, the most destructive in Sullivan County's history. The buildings to the right are all still standing, most virtually unchanged, today.

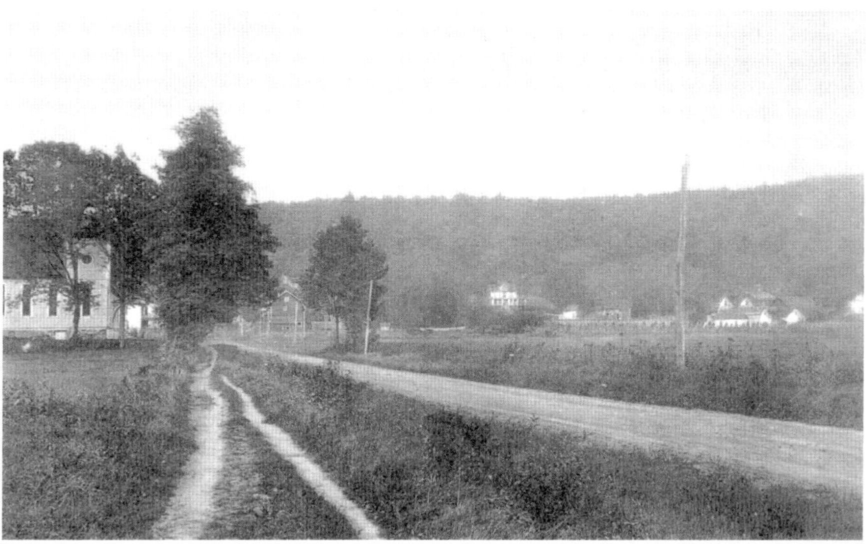

The western side of Sullivan County, especially the area along the Delaware River, was unaffected by the changes underway elsewhere. The hamlet of Cochecton in the upper Delaware Valley, like the aforementioned Claryville in the upper Neversink Valley, was able to retain its rustic ambiance, despite the drastic changes that the center of the county was undergoing.

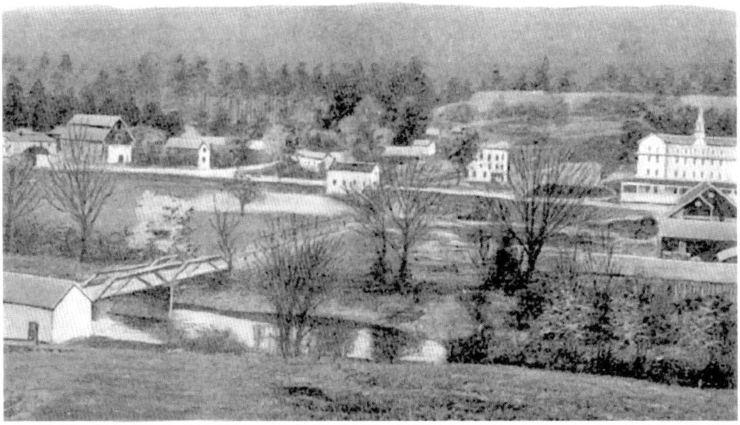

The hamlets of Lackawack (pictured), Montela and Eureka were displaced by the construction of the New York City Water Supply system, specifically by the Merriman Dam, which created the six-and-a-half-mile-long Rondout Reservoir. The reservoir comprises 2,052 acres and holds nearly fifty billion gallons. The three communities ceased to exist after their residents were forced to move elsewhere. *Photo courtesy of Time and the Valleys Museum, Grahamsville.*

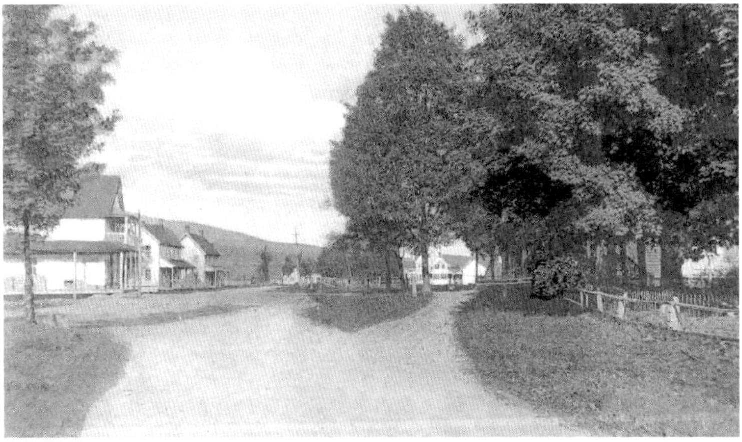

Montela was a small community before it was, like its neighbors, obliterated by the reservoir. The construction project began in 1937, halted during the war years and took decades to complete, finally wrapping up in 1954. *Photo courtesy of Time and the Valleys Museum, Grahamsville.*

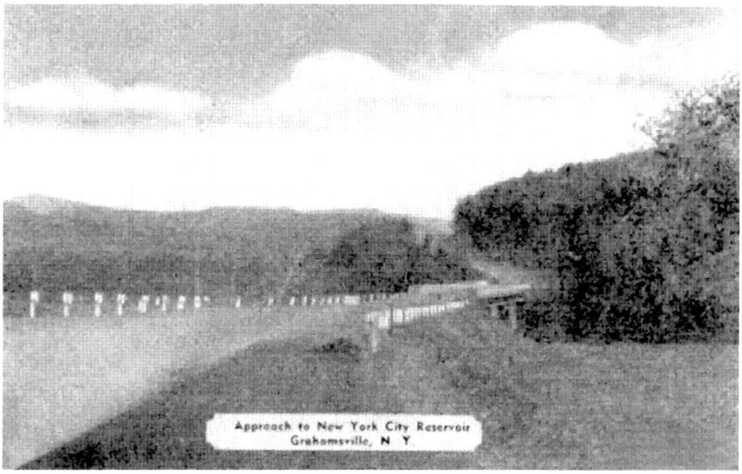

Like its larger neighbor the Rondout, the Neversink Reservoir displaced a number of people, including the communities of Neversink and Bittersweet. Neversink relocated, but Bittersweet faded away. The Neversink Reservoir was built between 1941 and 1953. It is about five miles long and contains nearly thirty-five billion gallons when at full capacity.

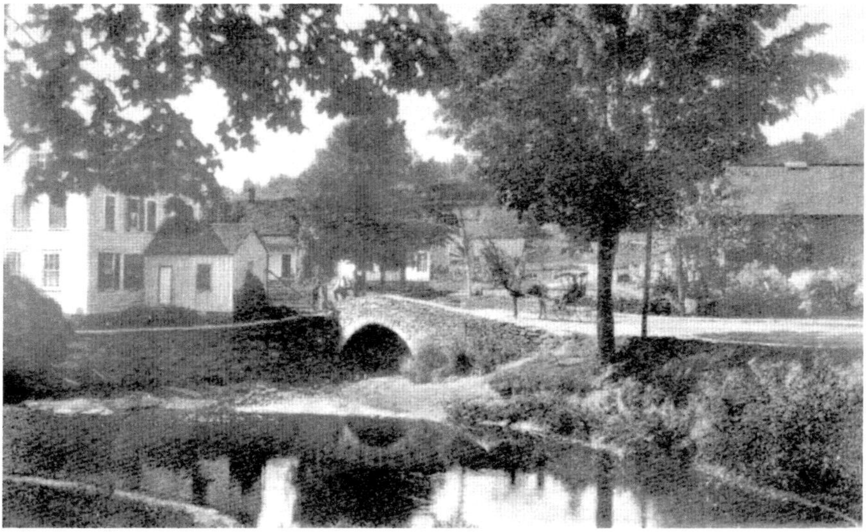

The village of Jeffersonville is the county's newest incorporated village, receiving its official charter in 1924. Originally settled mainly by German and Swiss immigrants after businessman Solomon Royce placed ads for cheap parcels of land in German-language newspapers, the area was once known as Winkelried. Jeffersonville was once home to its own German-language newspaper, the *Volksblatt*. The stone arch bridge shown at right was likely built around 1850 by the same masons who constructed the larger bridge nearby at Kenoza Lake.

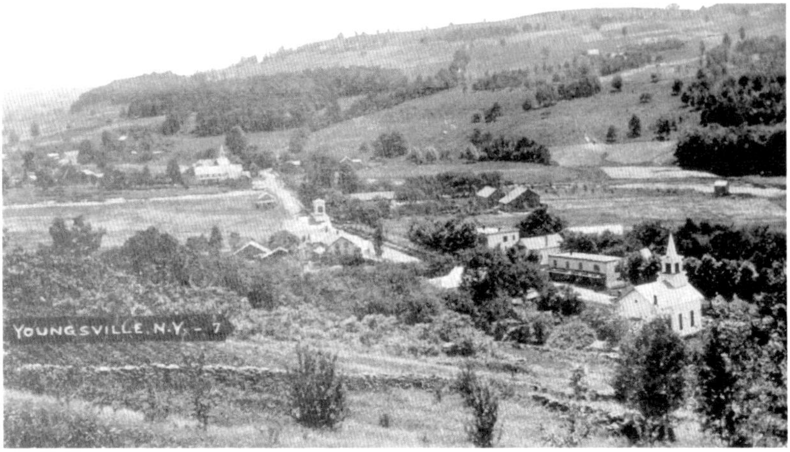

Youngsville was home to a number of hotels throughout the county's transition to the Golden Age but escaped the drastic changes most other communities witnessed. The hamlet's hotels remained small, and Youngsville mostly managed to retain its rural charm. One of its small resorts, the Mount Sunset Farm, accommodated twenty-five in 1940 and advertised that it was "an ideal place for Gentile vacationists." The German cooking included "home made bread, delicious pastries, and chicken twice weekly."

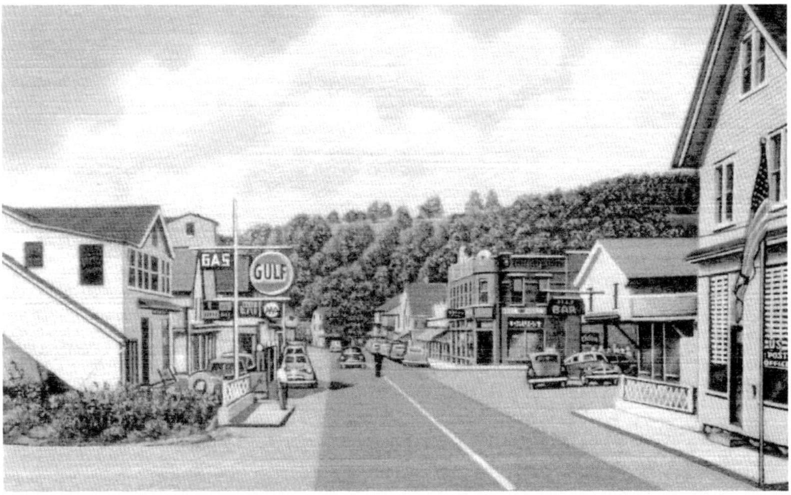

Parksville, one of the county's oldest communities, has suffered more than its share of ups and downs. Its heyday might have come while the Liberty Highway was in full swing. Originally designated such in 1918 by R.H. Johnston, an official of the White Motor Car Company, the Liberty Highway ran along State Route 4 and was the preferred route for the company to ship vehicles from its Cleveland, Ohio plant to New York City. Soon, other car manufacturers, including Buick, Hudson and Maxwell, were also using the road, which ran right through Parksville. State Route 4 became Route 17, and when that road was rebuilt as the Quickway in the late 1950s, the hamlet was bypassed.

Chapter 5

THE FORTRESS HOTEL

The hotels of the Golden Age featured two of the largest and most famous resorts in the world—the Concord in Kiamesha Lake and Grossinger's in Liberty—but not many of the more than five hundred hotels in the area were of that magnitude. There were many large facilities, comprising hundreds of acres and dozens of buildings, golf and tennis courts, nightclubs and coffee shops. There were also many smaller places, set on just a few acres, with two or three buildings and not much more than the owner's extended family on staff.

These smaller establishments were the hotels that contributed greatly to the surrounding communities. After all, they could not offer their guests big-name entertainment every night, and they didn't feature shops and stores on their premises. Guests had to go into town at least occasionally and patronized movie theatres, restaurants, gas stations, souvenir shops, hair salons and clothing stores.

As these small hotels began to struggle and close down, businesses in the surrounding communities suffered. Soon, entire villages were struggling. The larger hotels, meanwhile, began to become more and more self-sufficient. The concept of "the fortress hotel" was solidly in place by the 1960s, as more and more resorts offered their guests all-inclusive packages that gave them little reason to ever leave the premises.

The massive hotels that survived the end of the Golden Age typically included hair salons and barbershops, clothing stores, sundry shops and other businesses right on the grounds. The Concord even featured an Oriental rug dealer on site, as well as its own gas station.

The *New York Times* made note of "the fortress hotel" phenomenon in an article in its July 20, 1958 edition, attributing a struggling economy in the county at least in part to it.

Now, the big hotels have vanished, and as painful and as tragic as it once seemed, their disappearance has represented another transition in the evolution of tourism in the area. The days of the "fortress hotel" are history, and so are the days when the hotel industry spent more than $4.1 million in new construction each year (a figure reported in the *Times* in June 1955). The 750,000 hotel guests in the county once dropped upward of $55 million here in a single summer (as the *New York Times* estimated occurred in 1954), but that was a long time ago.

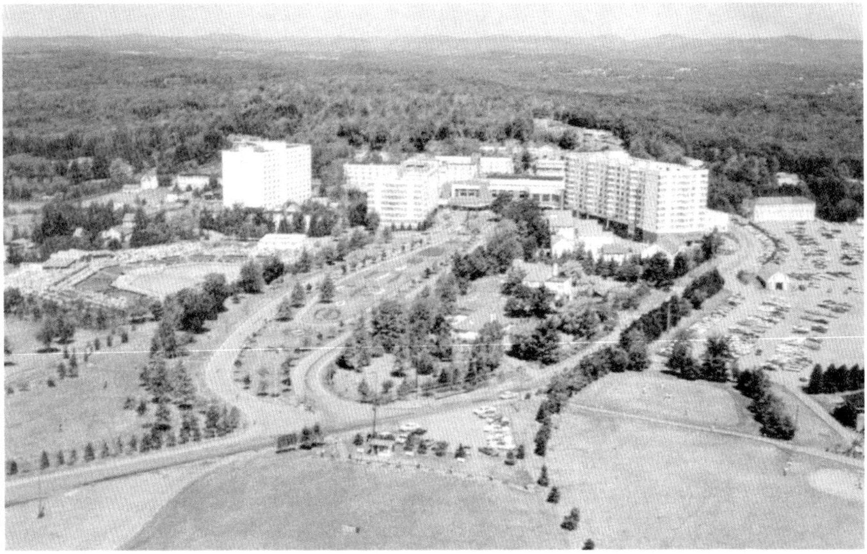

The concept of the fortress hotel was typified by the Concord, which was located on beautiful Kiamesha Lake but could have been anywhere, since it made little use of its location. The Concord offered forty-five holes of golf, forty tennis courts, a ski hill, indoor and outdoor pools and skating rinks and an Imperial Room nightclub that held fifteen hundred. The hotel owned its own vending machines, operated its own laundry and even owned its own gas station.

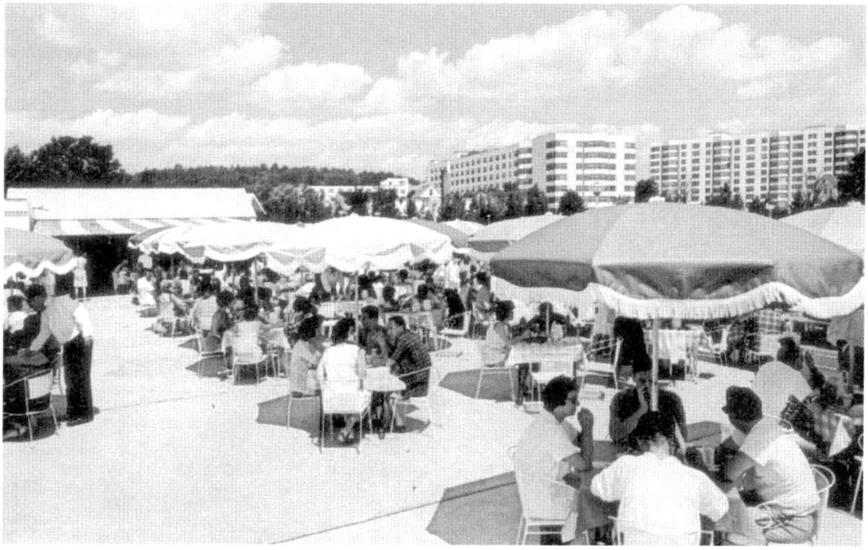

Once guests arrived at the fortress hotel, there was no reason for them to leave. All meals were paid for in the package deal and therefore taken at the hotel. Entertainment was provided nightly, and all sports facilities were located on the premises. Most large hotels featured valet parking, and guests didn't even know where their cars were parked during their stay.

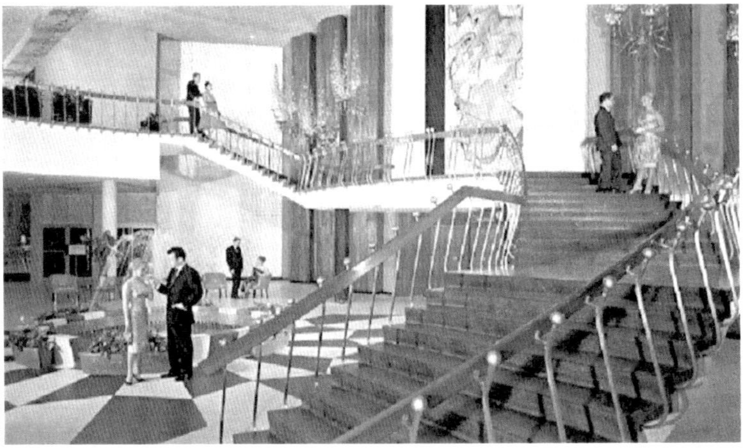

The Concord lobby, featuring its magnificent "stairway to nowhere," an architectural signature of Morris Lapidus, who designed most of the hotel's more recent buildings. Arthur Winarick had seen the work Lapidus had done for the Novak family at the Fountainbleu in Miami Beach and brought him north.

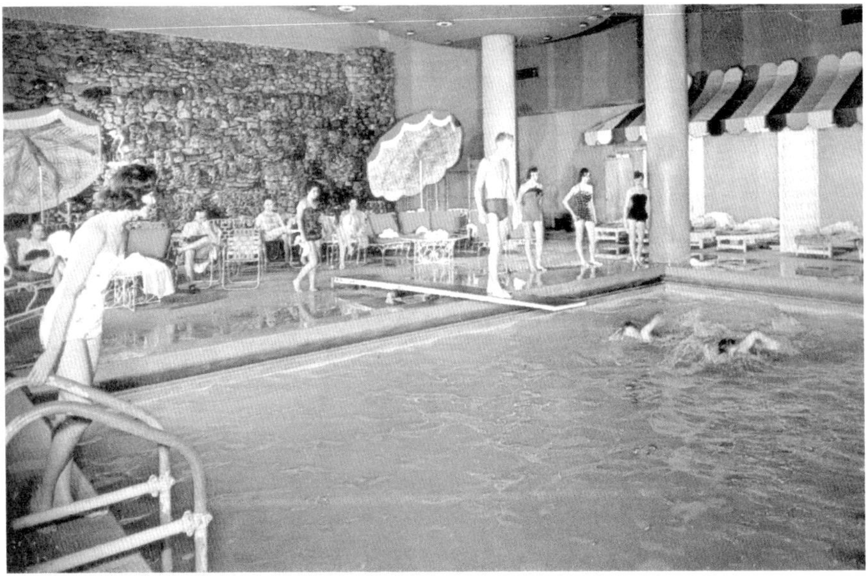

By the early 1960s, indoor pools were obligatory at Catskill hotels, and many smaller hotel owners went bankrupt building them. One owner told the *New York Times*, "People always ask if you have an indoor pool when they call for reservations, even if they don't swim. If you say 'no,' they hang up." Not surprisingly, the Concord was a pioneer in this area.

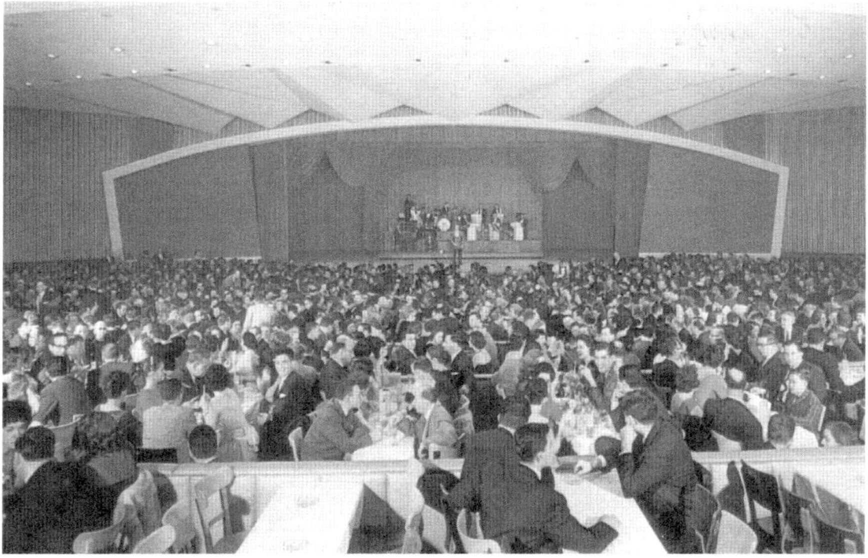

The Concord's Imperial Room was once the largest nightclub in the world. It regularly featured some of the biggest names in entertainment and was just one more reason why guests never had to leave the hotel.

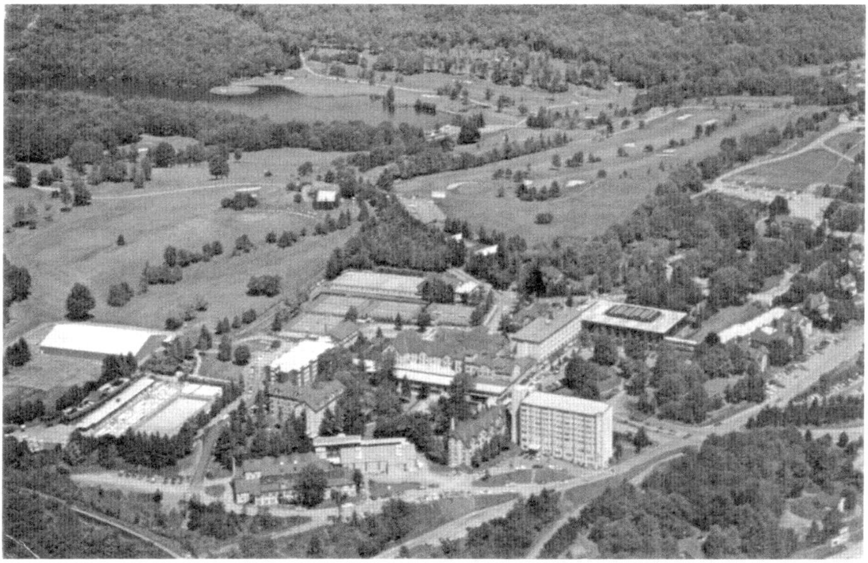

Grossinger's may not have been as large as the Concord, but it had a certain charm that its bigger rival could never match. It featured twenty-seven holes of golf, including an eighteen-hole layout rated among the best in the state, and regularly attracted celebrities from the world of sports and entertainment. It also had its own post office for many years, a distinction the Concord could never boast.

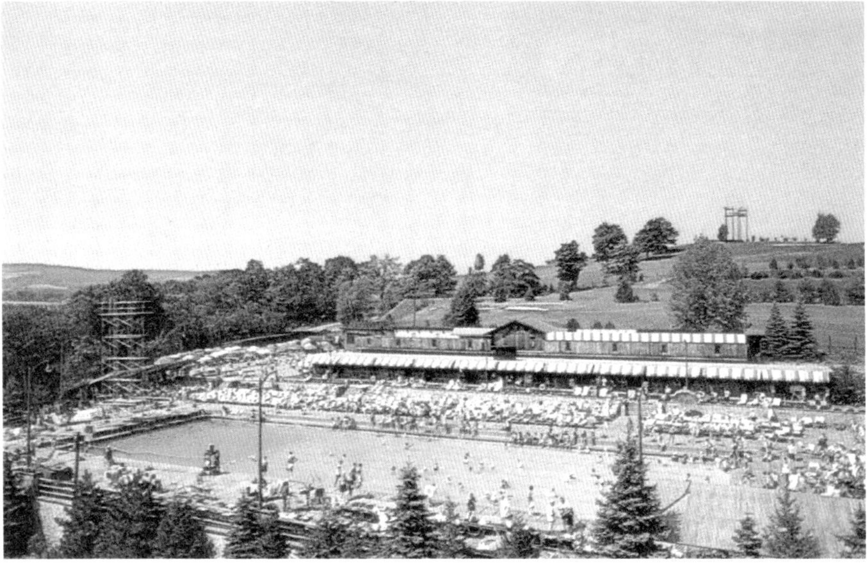

The outdoor pool at Grossinger's was always crowded, at least around the deck. It seemed that many more guests at Sullivan County hotels sat around the pool than ever actually swam in the pool. If guests were relaxing by the pool, they weren't spending their money in downtown shops.

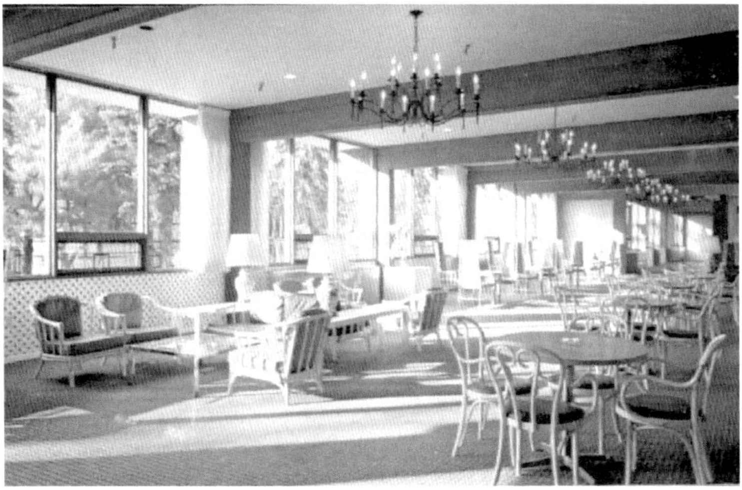

When there were hundreds of smaller hotels in Sullivan County, many of the guests would head into town on a rainy or cool day, taking in a movie or shopping. The indoor pool and the enclosed veranda, such as this very inviting one at Grossinger's, changed all that.

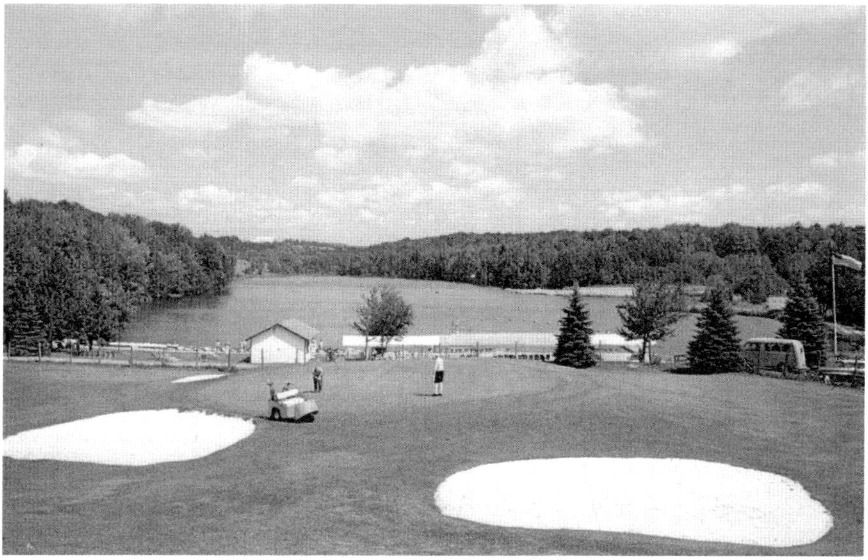

Grossinger's main golf course has long been the gold standard of Sullivan County courses. Even after the Concord opened its Monster, an impossible test for the average golfer, the Grossinger's course was usually rated the top course in the area and among the best in the state.

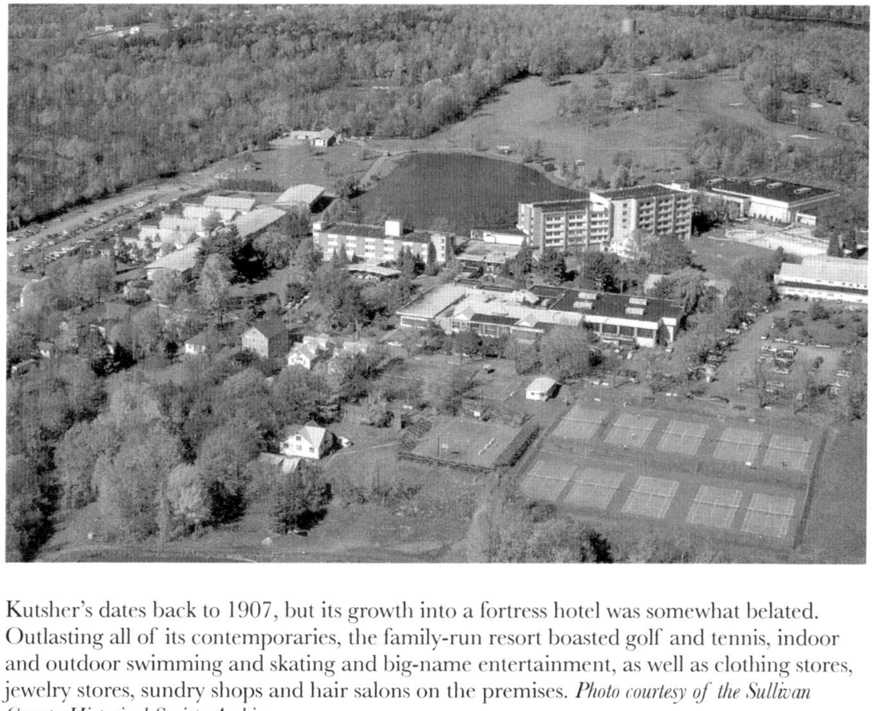

Kutsher's dates back to 1907, but its growth into a fortress hotel was somewhat belated. Outlasting all of its contemporaries, the family-run resort boasted golf and tennis, indoor and outdoor swimming and skating and big-name entertainment, as well as clothing stores, jewelry stores, sundry shops and hair salons on the premises. *Photo courtesy of the Sullivan County Historical Society Archives.*

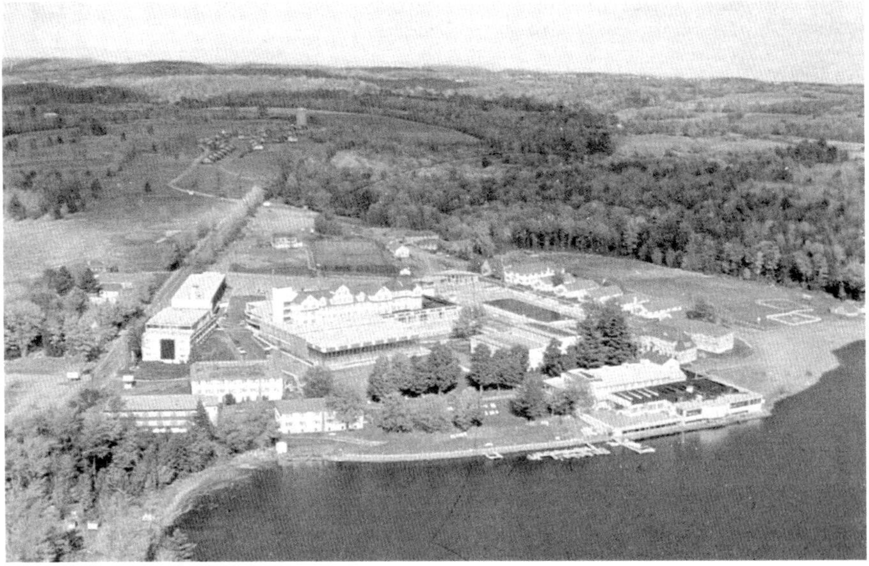

The Laurels on Sackett Lake was one of the earliest fortress hotels in the county. It was also the first to close. It once offered guests entertainers such as Sam Cooke and, in 1964, invested $2 million in improvements, including an indoor pool. It was bankrupt by the mid-1970s.

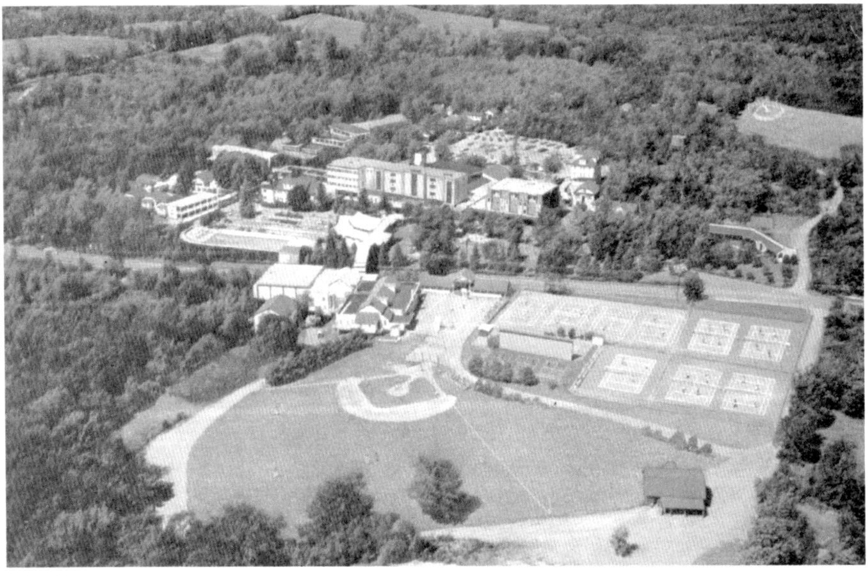

The Brickman, founded in 1910, had grown to over three hundred rooms by the time it was sold to the Siddha Yoga Dam for an Ashram. The Brickman was perhaps the first Sullivan County hotel to employ African Americans in any number. It was the favorite Catskills hangout of Jerry Seinfeld while he was learning his craft as a standup comedian.

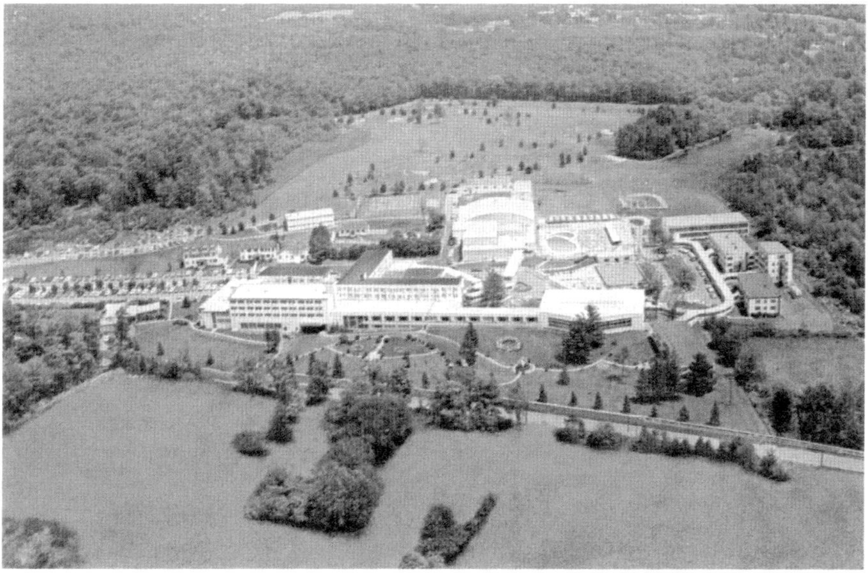

The Pines in South Fallsburg was a classic fortress hotel. The area had once been home to hundreds of hotels, and the hamlet prospered because of them. As the hotels closed down, the adjacent community struggled economically, and the hotels that remained found it necessary to segregate themselves from their surroundings. This was the ultimate tragedy of the fortress hotel movement. *Photo courtesy of the Sullivan County Historical Society Archives.*

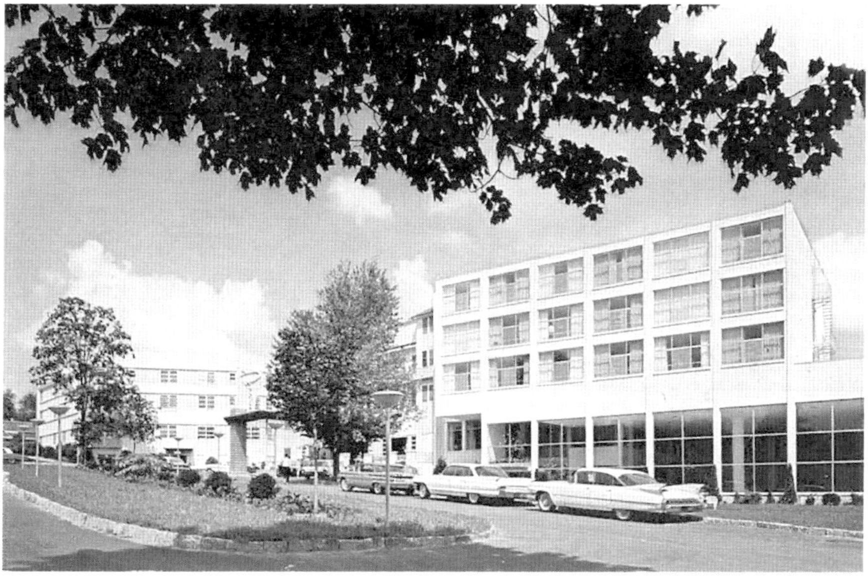

The Raleigh continued to grow into the 1980s and managed to stay afloat longer than most of the Sullivan County hotels. It was never as large as some but certainly qualified as a fortress hotel during its last decade of operation.

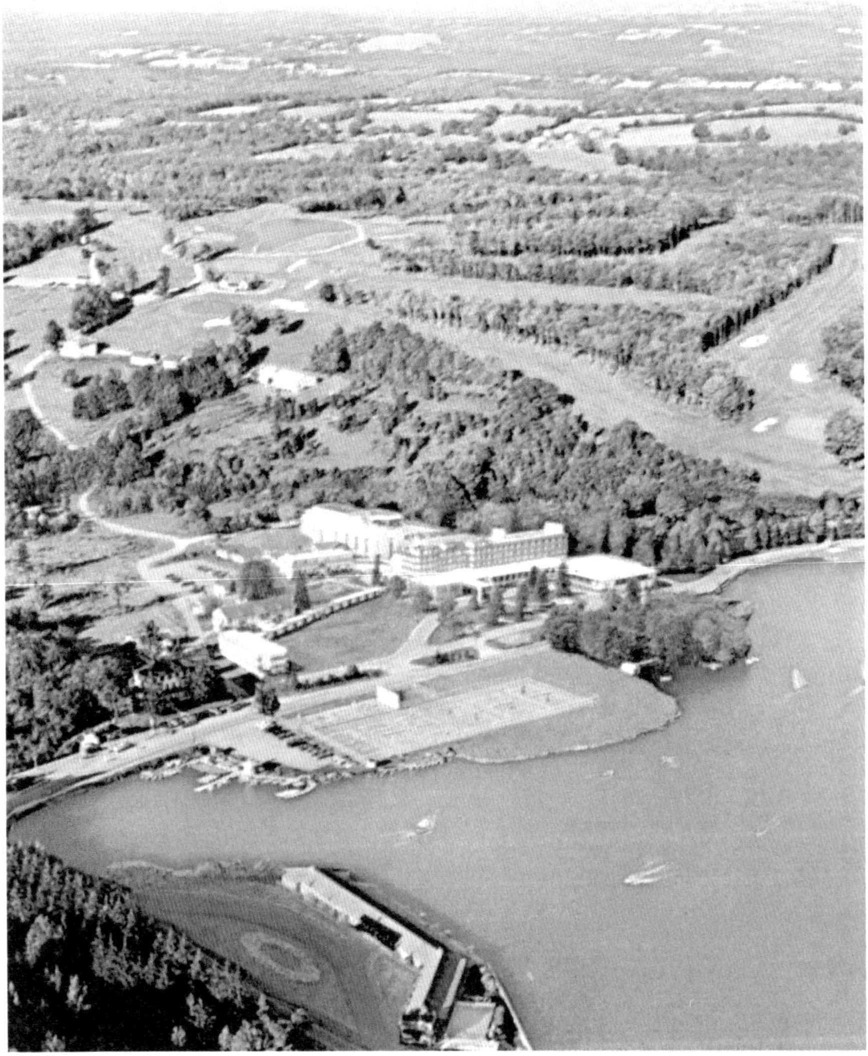

The Stevensville, located on picturesque Swan Lake, struggled for many years before finally closing down. Like most of its contemporaries, it featured eighteen holes of golf, indoor and outdoor tennis and swimming and big-name entertainment. *Photo courtesy of the Sullivan County Historical Society Archives.*

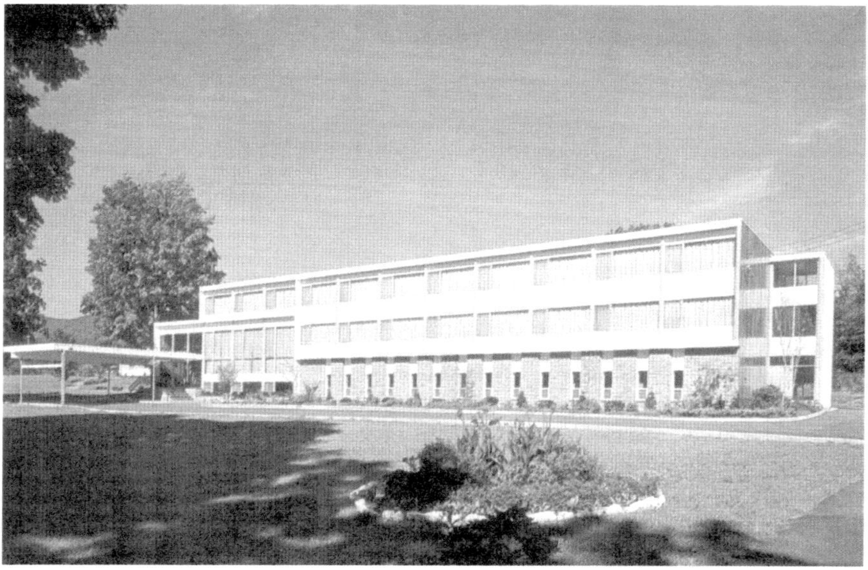

Despite its location far from the madding crowds in Spring Glen, the Homowack grew into a modern fortress hotel, complete with golf course, tennis courts, indoor and outdoor pools and nightclub.

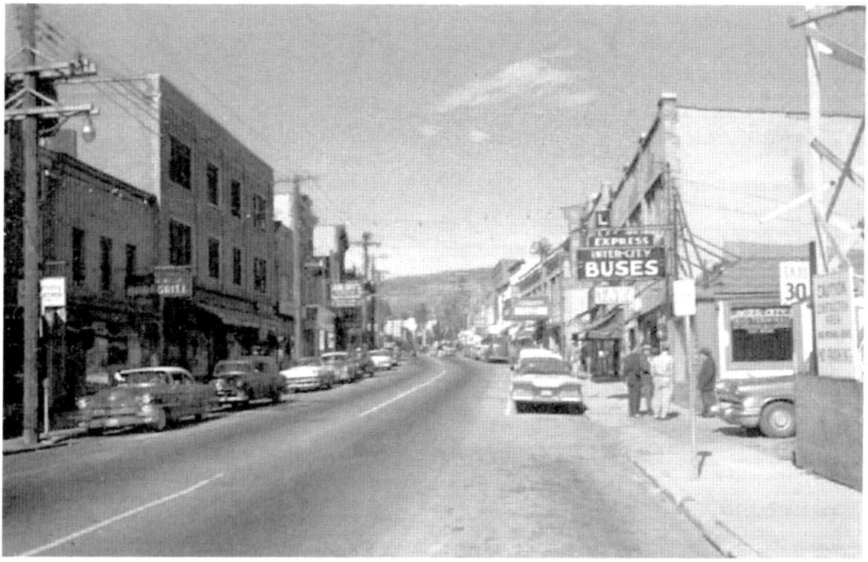

As the smaller hotels closed beginning in the mid-1960s, the economies of the neighboring communities struggled. Liberty was a good example, as its Main Street suffered when many of the surrounding hotels closed, beginning with the Young's Gap in 1967, and Grossinger's became more and more self-contained.

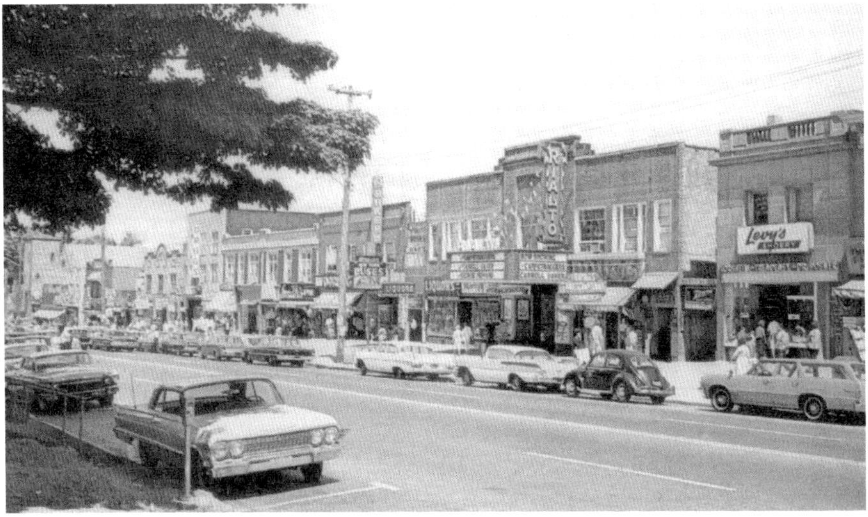

Monticello's Broadway thrived through the 1960s but began a downward trend as the decade came to a close. Where it was once common for pedestrians to be shoulder to shoulder on the village's sidewalks until late at night, before long the village was closed up tight by 9:00 p.m.

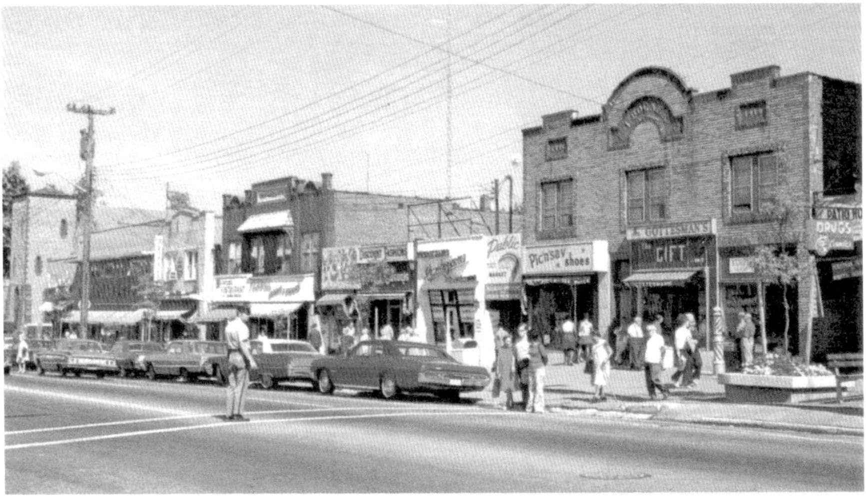

Even the influx of chain stores, such as the Woolworth's and National Shoes (left), could not slow the demise of Monticello's main business district once the Golden Age ended.

Chapter 6

AFTER THE FALL

Although many once thought that it was unlikely, if not impossible, Sullivan County has survived the demise of the hotel era. The Golden Age is now nothing more than a distant memory, and with each passing year fewer and fewer residents are around who remember the heyday of the mountains.

But the area remains vibrant. Tourism is alive and well, even without the hundreds of hotels of the Silver and Golden Ages. Tourists today are a different breed, as likely to be looking for bald eagles or places to kayak as for professional entertainment.

Heritage tourism has become an important part of the county's economy, with landmarks as diverse as the Roebling Bridge, the Minisink Battlefield, the Wurtsboro Airport and the Woodstock Festival site hosting hundreds of visitors each year.

There are still a few resorts around the county, including the Villa Roma, which has just rebuilt much of its main building following a devastating fire, and the Mountain View Resort, fashioned from one of the Mackenzie family mansions in Glen Spey. Bed-and-breakfasts now account for most of the county's accommodations, however, and a significant number of tourists own or rent second homes during their stays here.

Sullivan County officials have made a concerted effort to place the area in the vanguard of the "green technology" movement, and eco-tourism also promises to play an important role in the future economy of the region.

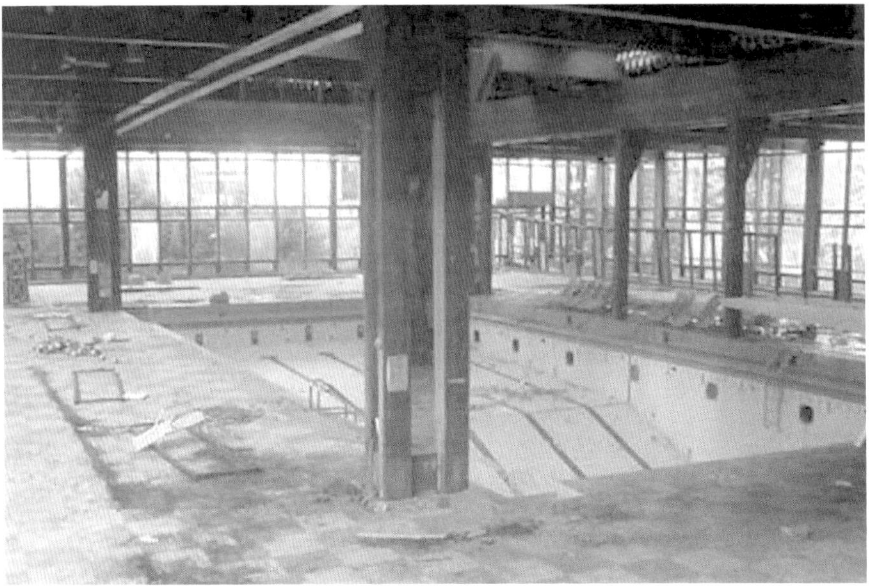

When the Grossinger family sold the famed resort, it was the beginning of the end. New owners never came through with an ambitious rebuilding plan, and most of the hotel's once magnificent buildings were allowed to decay. This is the indoor pool.

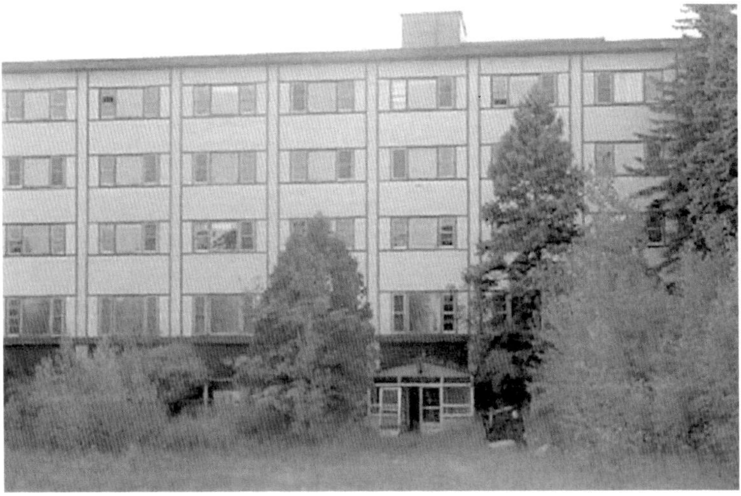

Grossinger's Jennie G. Building was the last word in hotel accommodations in its day, but it has been severely neglected of late. This is how it looked as the twentieth century came to a close.

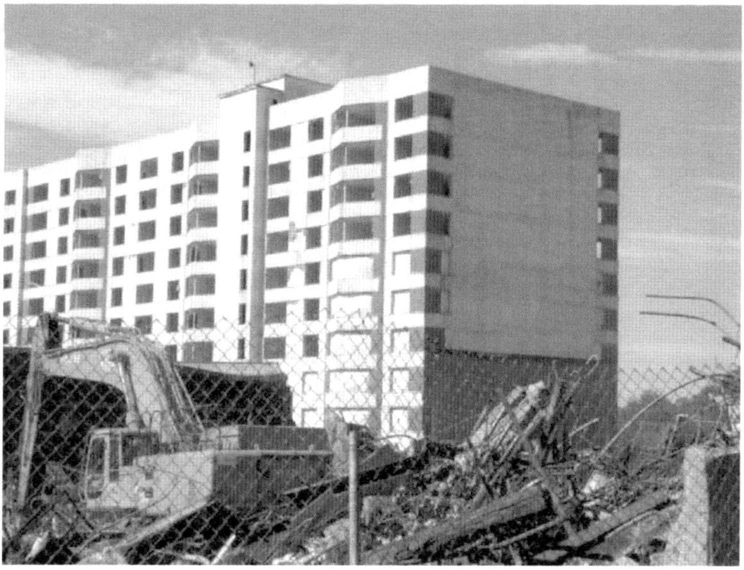

The sprawling complex that was once the Concord has been totally demolished, save for a few of the golf-related buildings. This Lapidus-designed building was one of the last to fall.

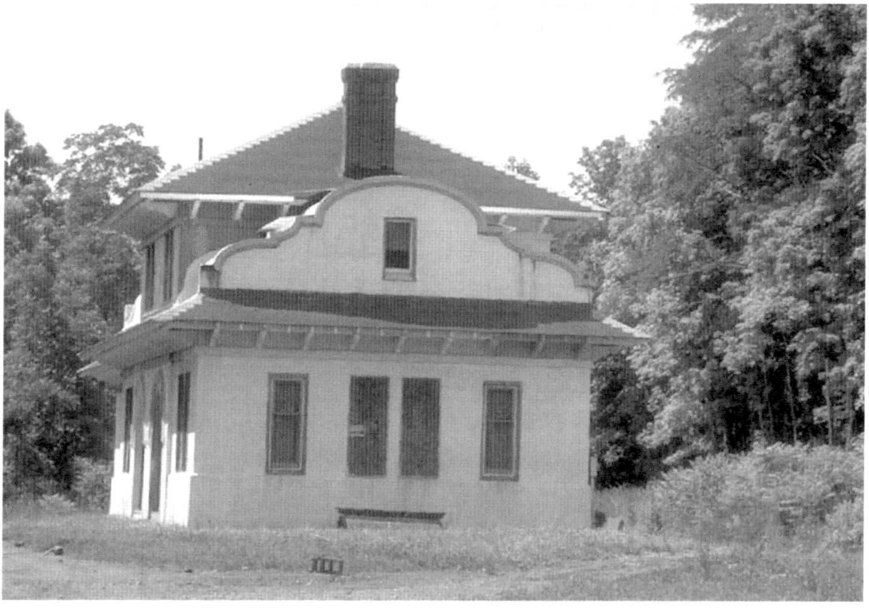

Some landmarks from the region's heyday were not torn down. The High View station, still the epitome of Sullivan County Mission styling, was adapted to reuse as a private residence.

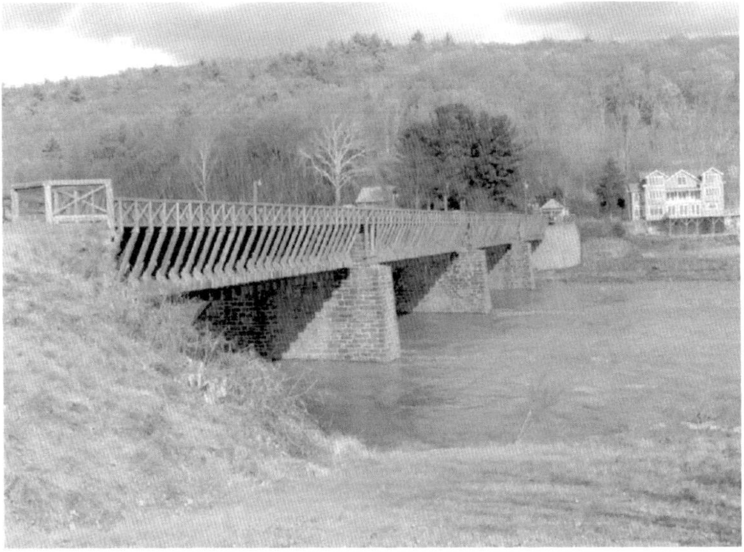

The National Park Service has completely and faithfully restored Roebling's Delaware Aqueduct to its original condition. The structure once heralded a new era in transportation in a heavily industrialized county. Today, it is one of the linchpins of a heritage tourism–based economy.

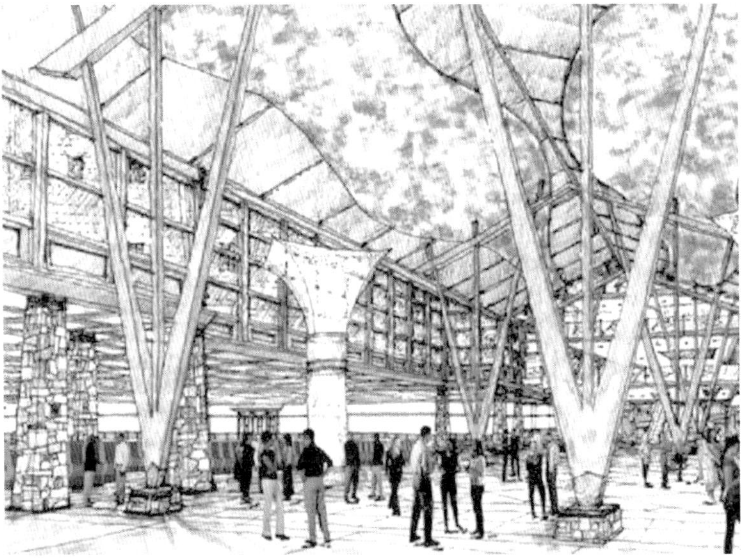

While Monticello Raceway has had its successes and failures over fifty years of operation, it is still a viable attraction. The track's owner, Empire Resorts, has coupled with developer Louis Cappelli to propose a modern, luxurious entertainment complex, including a harness track, at the site of the Concord.

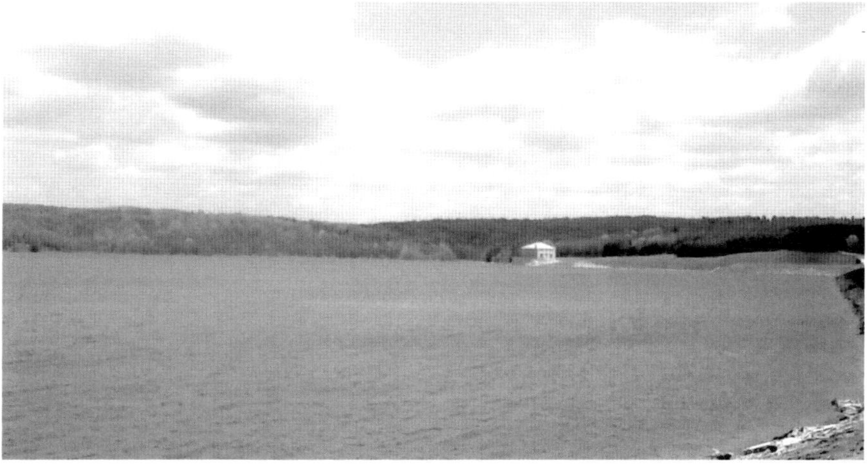

The New York City Water Supply reservoirs provide recreational opportunities for fishermen willing to pay for special permits and have been mostly a positive addition to the region.

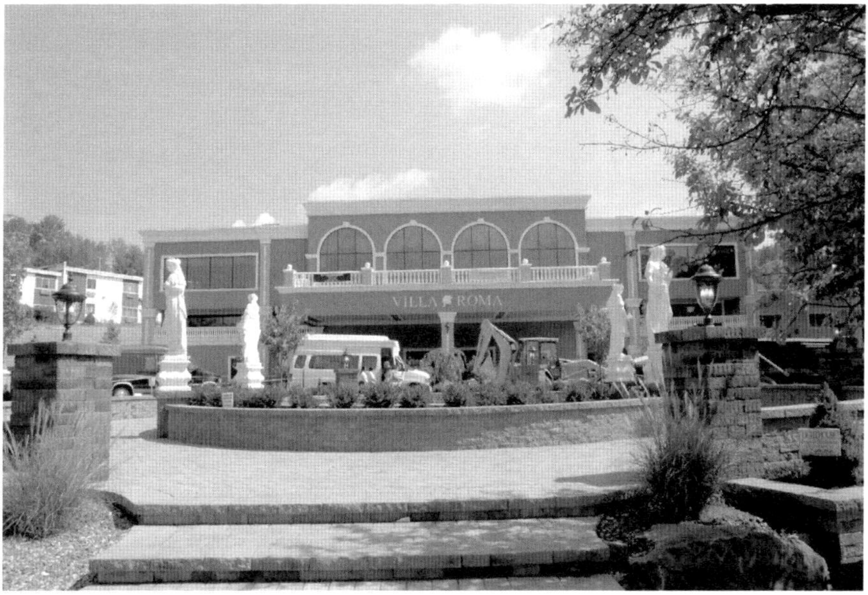

The Villa Roma resort in Callicoon remains one of the region's most successful hotels. Featuring a picturesque and challenging golf course and specializing in time shares, the resort has thrived. It recently rebuilt much of its main building after a devastating fire. *Photo courtesy of the* Sullivan County Democrat *newspaper.*

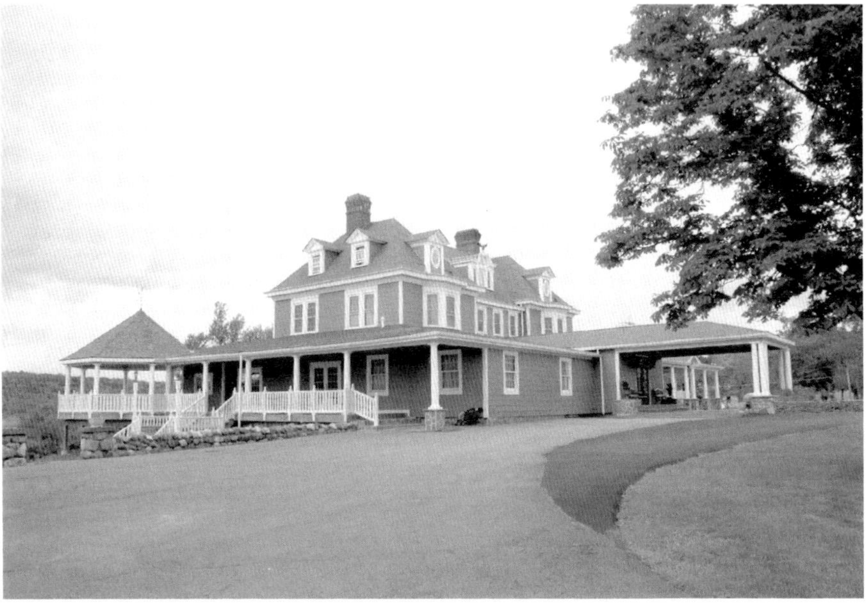

The Mountain View Resort in Glen Spey recently opened its doors, unveiling the newly restored Ardmore mansion that had once belonged to the Mackenzie family. Previous owners had modernized the structure, obscuring much of its original charm. *Photo courtesy of Mountain View Resort Archives.*

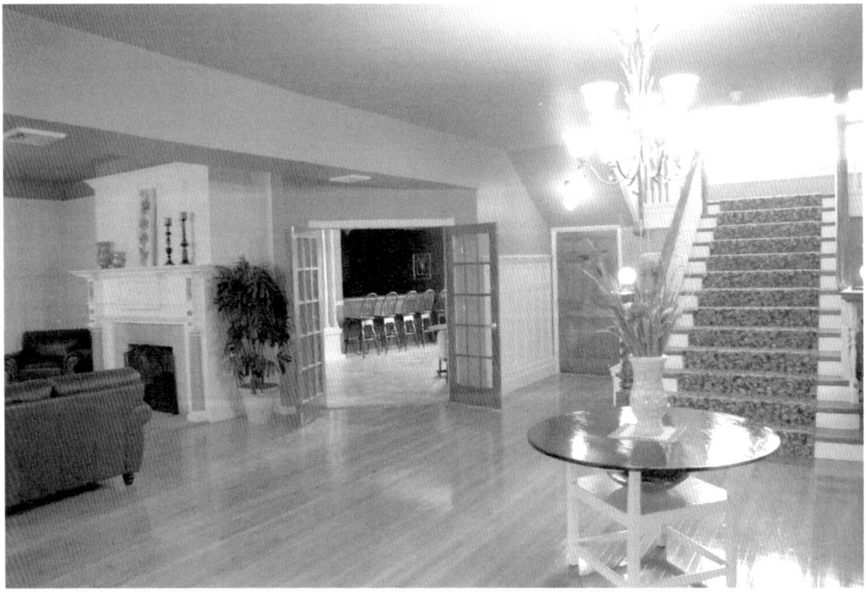

The county is in desperate need of resort accommodations, so hopes are high that the Mountain View will prove a successful operation. It is a beautiful location for weddings and other similar affairs. *Photo courtesy of Mountain View Resort Archives.*

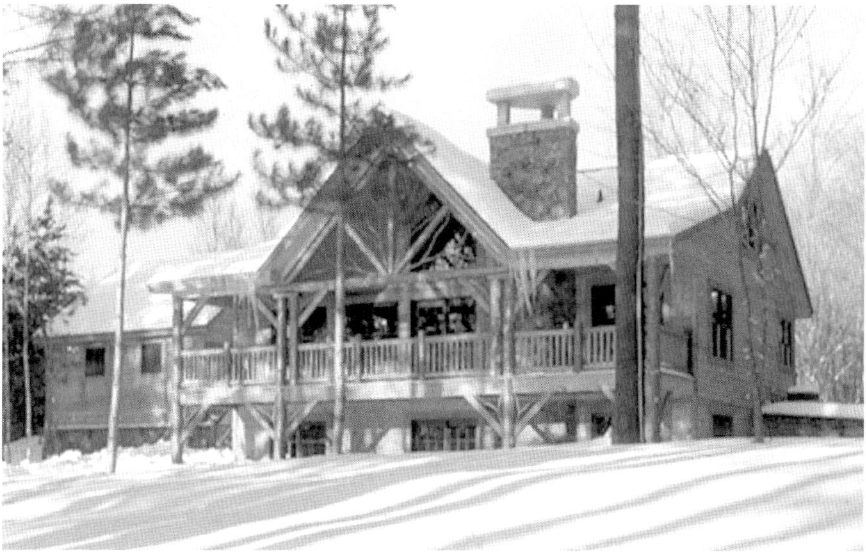

Second home owners and renters make up a large portion of Sullivan County's tourists these days. The homes at the Chapin Estate development, built on the property that once made up the hunting preserve of Chester W. Chapin, are at the highest end of the spectrum.

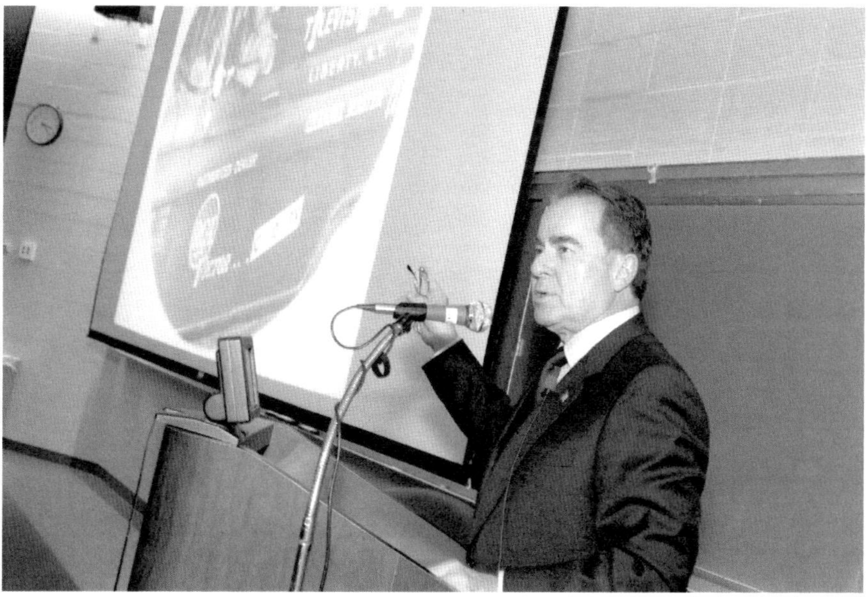

Local businessman Alan Gerry, who amassed a fortune in the cable television industry, has set about to construct world-class performing arts and museum venues at the site of the Woodstock Music Festival in Bethel. These attractions will be the linchpin of the new Sullivan County tourism industry.

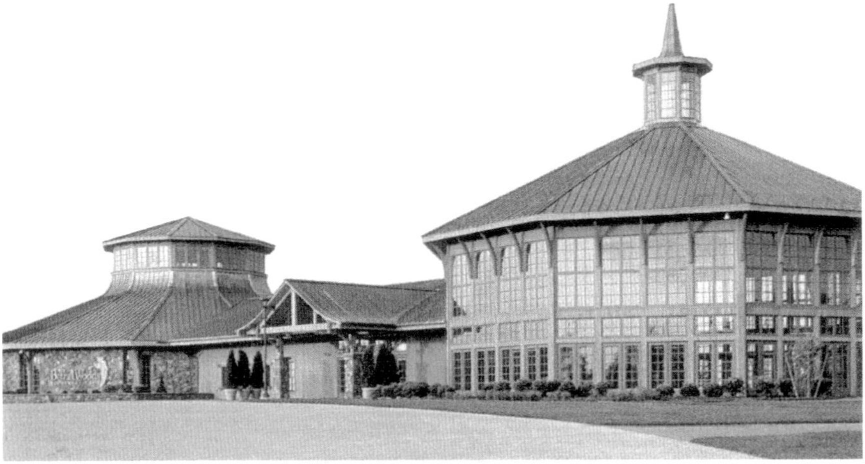

The Museum at Bethel Woods not only celebrates the Woodstock Music Festival, but it also interprets the changes that occurred in the nation during the 1960s. It is a state-of-the-art interactive museum and, with top-quality management, will only get better.

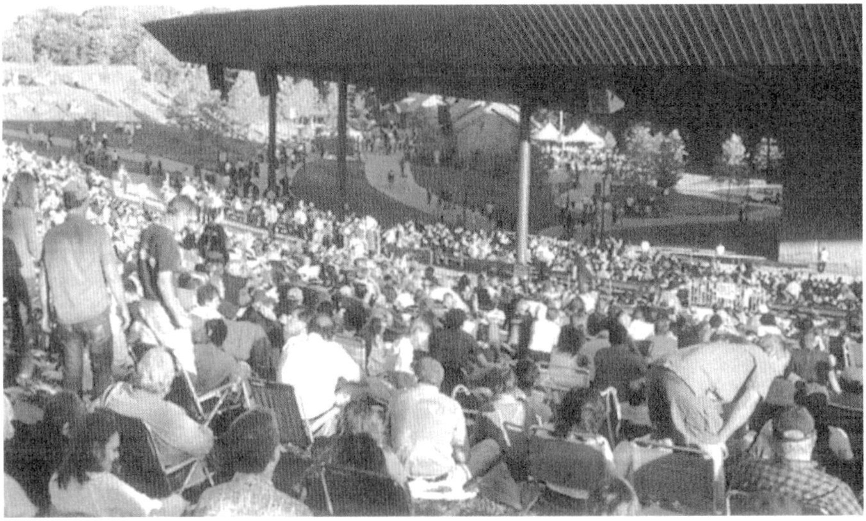

The Performing Arts Center at Bethel Woods is a state-of-the-art facility that gets better each season. It has already hosted acts as diverse as the Jonas Brothers; Brad Paisley; the Goo Goo Dolls; Crosby, Stills, Nash and Young; the New York Philharmonic; and the Boston Pops.

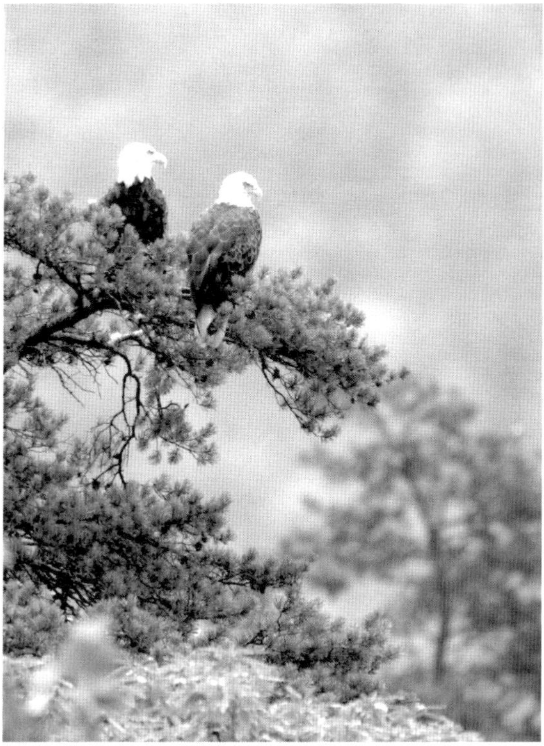

Right: The bald eagle was once an endangered species but began to thrive in Sullivan County's wilderness. Now, hundreds of visitors come to the upper Delaware region each winter to observe the magnificent raptors in their natural habitat.

Below: Sullivan County officials have announced their intention to become leaders in the green technology movement. BUZZ Enterprises in Woodridge has quietly been in the vanguard of the effort, designing, building, selling and repairing electric and other alternative fuel vehicles for several years now.

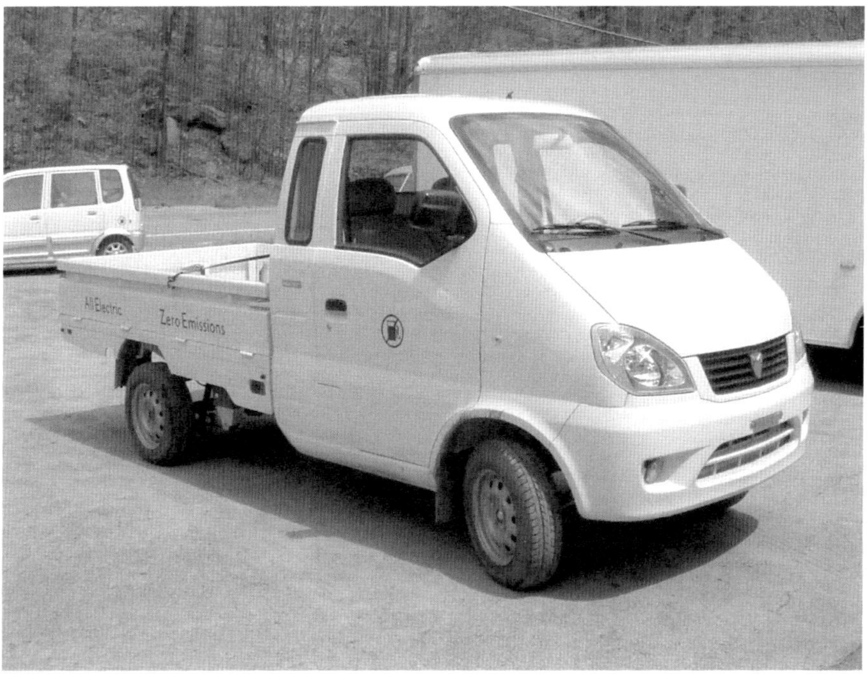

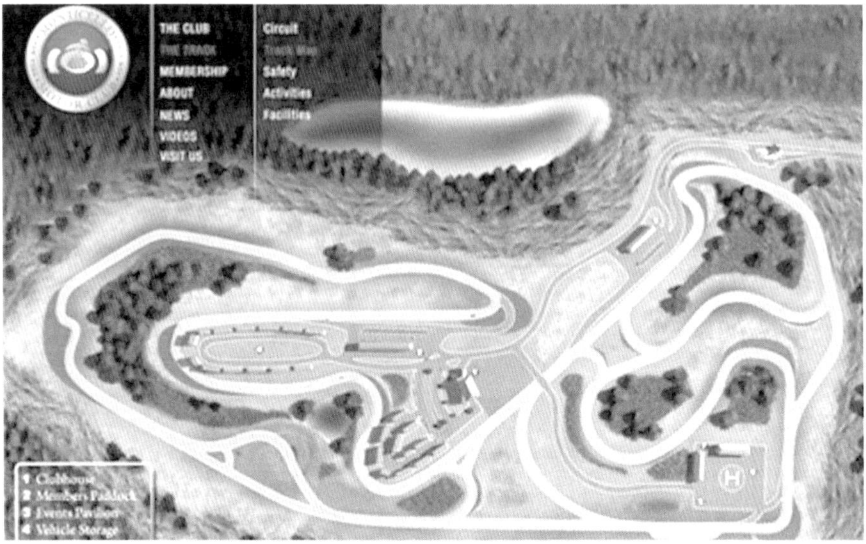

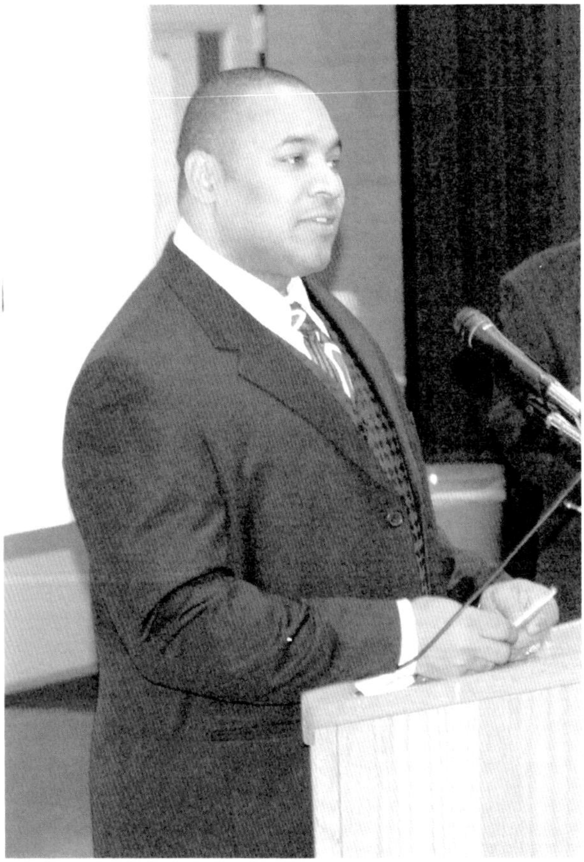

Above: The Monticello Motor Club, which began operation in 2008, could be a major asset for the county. Catering to very upscale car enthusiasts, the club opened its multi-configured track in 2008, and has announced plans to eventually include a luxurious clubhouse and other amenities.

Left: The village of Monticello continues to face challenges, including a shrinking tax base and a deteriorating infrastructure. The village made history recently by electing Gordon Jenkins the first African American mayor in Sullivan County's history. Jenkins grew up in the village and knows its problems firsthand.

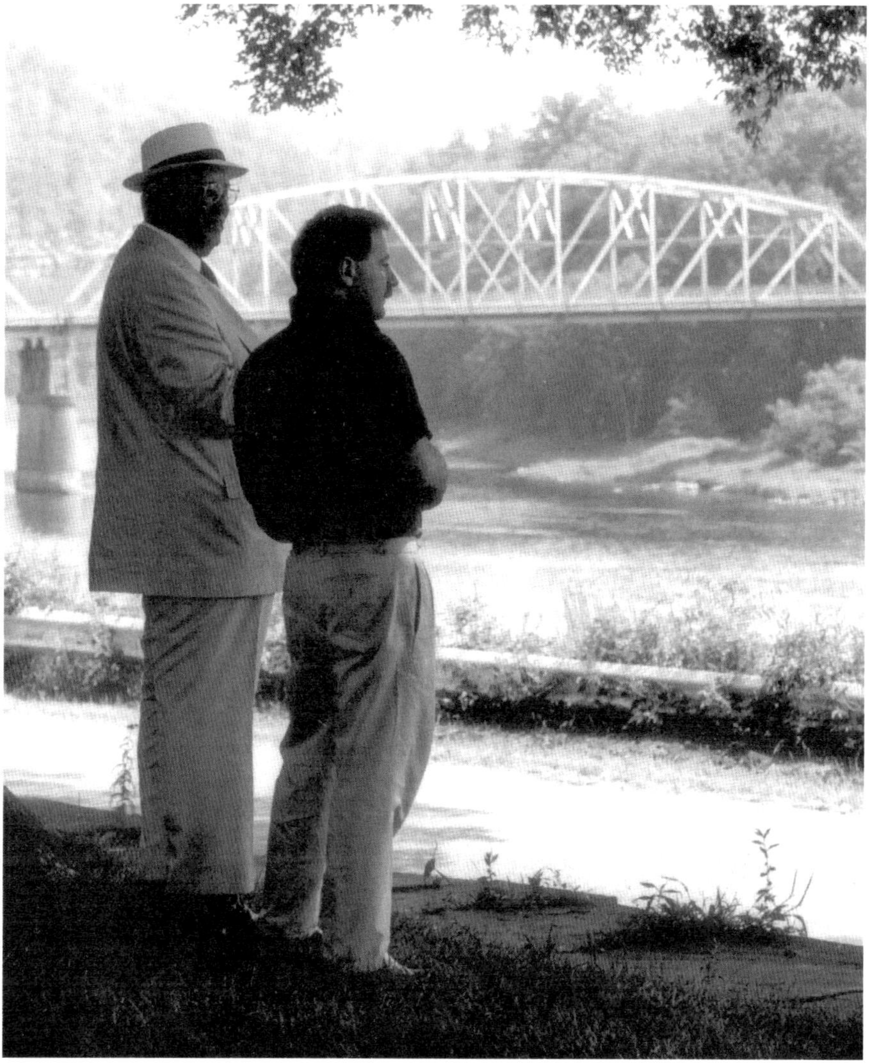

Monticello native Lawrence H. Cooke, pictured here with the author in 1991, was the son of county court judge George L. Cooke, who presided over some of the most high-profile cases in Sullivan County history. Lawrence served as Thompson supervisor before ascending to the bench himself, eventually reaching New York State's highest court, the Court of Appeals, where he served as chief judge until his retirement. Cooke was the second Monticello resident to serve as chief judge. William B. Wright held that position in 1848.

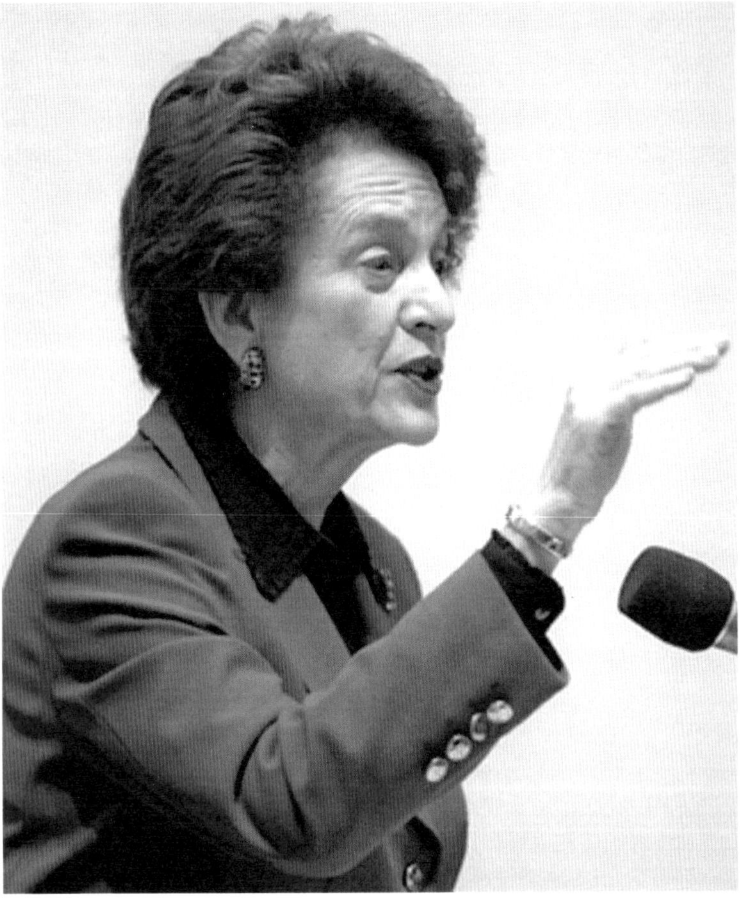

Judith Smith Kaye attended a one-room schoolhouse in Maplewood while her family operated a farm there. The family moved to Monticello and opened a clothing store, where Kaye often worked. She became a highly respected attorney and jurist, eventually serving as chief judge of the New York State Court of Appeals. She was the third judge from Monticello to hold the post.